BRUSH DIESEL LOCOMOTIVES 1940~78

BRUSH DIESEL LOCOMOTIVES 1940~78

GEORGE TOMS

First Published 1978.

©

**Turntable Publications and
The Transport Publishing Company 1978.**

**ISBN 0 902844 48 2
0 903839 31 8**

**PRINTED IN GREAT BRITAIN FOR THE PUBLISHERS
BY
CLIFFORD WHITTAKER, BOROUGH PRESS,
MOSSLEY, LANCASHIRE, ENGLAND.**

CONTENTS

INTRODUCTION

This book has been written to portray the historical side of Brush locomotives produced between 1940 and 1977. It outlines the Company's initial efforts to break into the diesel-electric locomotive market and the eventual recognition of Brush as a leading builder by the mid-1960s.

The Brush register of locomotives is followed in approximate chronological order and in doing this Brush-built locomotives, some locomotives which Brush supplied equipment for, sub-contracted examples and joint Brush-Bagnall efforts are all included. Throughout the late fifties, sixties and seventies Brush supplied many items of electrical equipment to British Rail and overseas railways to such an extent as to be beyond the scope of this book. Brush Traction did not just build locomotives, it was (and still is) part of a larger concern producing a wide range of electrical products. Perhaps, due to the latter, records have been very short-lived and have been disposed of from time to time. This trend was of help to work in progress but not to the historian, and outside sources have been most helpful. Perhaps in a purely railway establishment this situation might not have occurred, as the railway tradition of retaining historical records is very strong.

One day the task of compiling the pre-diesel era will bear fruit, but that is some time away, with much research to be undertaken.

I must record my thanks to the following organisations and individuals for their willing help:

Industrial Railway Society
The Diesel and Electric Group
The Irish Railway Record Society
Loughborough Public Library
Brush Electrical Machines, Publicity Department
Coras Iompair Eireann
Rhodesia Railways
Ceylon Government Railways
British Steel Corporation
National Coal Board
Mr R. E. Dilley
Mr F. R. Kerr
Mr D. Carter
Mr F. H. Wood
Mr J. Howie
Peter Barnes
John Buckland
Brian Webb
and many others

Also I must thank Mr J. M. Durber of B.E.M. Ltd. for permission to use official photographs and to publish this account.

Finally thanks must go to my wife Peggy who, ably assisted by Sandra and Marion, typed the manuscript.

G. Toms
Loughborough
September 1977

1. No. 47.116 (D 1704), with copious exhaust haze in evidence, tackles the steepest part of Brentwood Bank at the head of a Liverpool Street — Norwich express on 16 April 1977. J.A. Howie.

EARLY DAYS

The variety of products which have emerged from the Falcon Works at Loughborough during the last 112 years is quite remarkable, ranging from horse-drawn omnibuses, transformers and electrical switchgear, to trams, trolleybuses and railway locomotives.

The works were founded in 1865 by Henry Hughes, a Loughborough engineer and timber merchant, who had established his business ten years previously in Derby Road. He bought seven acres of land opposite the Midland Station and goods yards, erected suitable buildings and established a rail link to the rear of the Station. The new works traded under the title "Henry Hughes and Comvany, Locomotive Engineers". Although the title suggested that only locomotives were built, right from the beginning railway coaches, wagons and horse-drawn tramcars were produced. It was a natural outlet for Henry Hughes' interests as a timber merchant. The year when Henry Hughes' first locomotive appeared was perhaps 1865, although its identity is rather obscure; certainly more than forty 0–4–0 saddle tanks were built during the first few years. It was also a period of expansion for the main line railways, in particular the Midland, and much business came Hughes' way. Following the 1870 Tramways Act which authorized local authorities to construct street tramways and operate mechanically propelled vehicles, even more business was undertaken, with steam tramway locomotives being constructed at Falcon Works. The first one went to Leicester Tramways in 1876 and another went to the Swansea & Mumbles Railway the following year.

Unfortunately during the late 1870s a decline in trade and over-capitalisation of the Company resulted in financial difficulties. In 1883 the Company was taken over by Norman Scott Russell and renamed "The Falcon Engineering and Car Works". Trade improved, the first horse-drawn omnibuses being introduced in 1885. Some forty-two Hughes and sixty-one Russell steam tram locomotives were built up to 1888.

By 1889 electric tramcars had become a practical proposition and the Company sought ways of entering this new market by contacting electrical concerns to fill in for their lack of electrical knowledge. The Anglo-American Brush Electric Light Corporation, which had been established in London in 1879, merged with the existing Company at the Falcon Works in 1889 and continued the expansion of the site under the new title "Brush Electrical Engineering Company Limited". This merger introduced many electrical interests to Loughborough, but tramcars, steam locomotives, coaches and wagons emerged in ever-increasing numbers, effectively combining the constituent companies' interests on this one site.

2. A single-deck horse bus of 1885.   Brush.

3. A Brush double-deck motor bus of 1904.   Brush.

4. Electric tramcars under construction at the Brush factory.
          Brush.

By the turn of the century the tramcar side of the business occupied five acres of new buildings, complete with internal railway tracks and an external interconnecting rail traverser, at the northern end of the shops. In 1912 the steam locomotive side of the business ended after a gradual decline. About 250 conventional steam locomotives had been built, in addition to the tram engines, but no accurate records have survived. Several small electric locomotives were produced between 1900 and 1917. Prior to 1914 the limitations of tramways began to be realised and the trolleybus idea was pursued, but the First World War and its aftermath prevented much work being undertaken until the 1920s. Trolleybus business was expanded, partly at the expense of railway work, until the 1940s when rail traction re-emerged as a major activity.

There was a slender thread which linked the old era with the new in the form of one of the works shunters, an 0–4–0 inside cylinder saddle tank named *Sprite* (Brush 283 of 1899), which had expired in 1938 in need of heavy repairs. This locomotive became the first Brush diesel as explained in the next chapter.

5. The link between the steam and diesel locomotive building eras was the 0-4-0 saddle tank *Sprite* (Brush 283 of 1899). It is seen here at Falcon Works in 1938, not long before it broke down beyond economic repair.   Rev. E. Boston.

6. Tramcar bodies were loaded onto flat railway wagons for delivery to many customers. These open-top double-deckers were for Croydon Corporation. The direct factory rail link was invaluable.   Brush.

THE DIESEL ERA BEGINS

During the 1930s the Company had watched trial working of the 350 bhp diesel-electric shunter, particularly on the London Midland & Scottish Railway, and decided to venture again into the locomotive building field, by combining their electrical experience with the oil engine business acquired in 1938. The most obvious choice at that time was to use the old works 0–4–0 saddle tank named *Sprite,* which had just broken down and was in need of heavy repairs. *Sprite* had already had some boiler tubes replaced, but was then found to be in need of extensive firebox repairs, through a large hole appearing there. Rather than reboiler or rebuild *Sprite* as a steam locomotive, Brush took the opportunity to convert her to diesel-electric in 1939.

The year 1939 also saw the Second World War break out, and this event probably prompted Brush to seek readily available components from within the Falcon Works. A discarded prototype engine was found, this being a two-cylinder horizontally-opposed type, developing 80 to 120 bhp at 375 to 500 rpm. It had been designed several years earlier and a four-cylinder version was fitted into several Dundee Harbour Trust ferry boats. An old d.c. generator was found and two tramcar traction motors unearthed from near the boiler house, where they had lain for several years. The latter were thought to be worth only their copper content as scrap, but a trial run on the electrical machines test proved them to be in sound working order.

The *Sprite* rebuild was taken in hand, and the boiler, cylinders, saddle tank and valve gear all removed. Various equipment layouts were tried, but only one was found to be reasonably satisfactory and this involved the engine being mounted transversely, immediately forward of the cab. This created two peculiar bulges in the bonnet, one each side of the locomotive, and within them were situated the rocker box covers, on the end of the cylinder casings. The crankshaft was therefore in line with the locomotive frames, while the main generator was directly coupled to the engine and mounted forward of it. Further forward lay the auxiliary equipment and fuel tanks. The engine could be started either electrically, or by compressed air from a reservoir. A peculiarly-shaped chimney housed part of the exhaust silencing equipment, perhaps one of the most unusually styled diesel exhausts seen in this country. The locomotive was believed to have been rated at around 80 bhp, the limiting factor being electrical output. *Sprite* was repainted green and given a klaxon horn in place of the steam whistle. It retained the original nameplates (now preserved), works plates and open-backed cab, although the latter received different front windows. The dumb buffers were also retained and side sheeting partly enclosed the area below the running board.

Sprite re-entered service in November 1940 and was reputed to be a very reliable performer around the works, being able to pull away smoothly with twelve loaded wagons. It continued in service until withdrawn in 1946 and was sold for scrap to a local firm called Johnsons.

7. *Sprite* seen working on the internal railway system at Falcon Works in November 1940, shortly after being rebuilt as the first Brush diesel-electric locomotive. Collection of A. Hutt.

The limited success of *Sprite* led Brush to develop their equivalent of the 0–6–0 diesel-electric shunter. The project was much delayed by the War, but an arrangement was secured by the Company with the London & North Eastern Railway through Sir Ronald Matthews, who was at the time Chairman of both Brush and the Railway. The Railway had built four 350 hp 0–6–0 diesel-electrics of modified English Electric design (8000–3, later BR 15000–3) at its Doncaster works during 1944/5 and the Brush version of these followed in 1947. The underframes and some mechanical parts were built at Doncaster, but the main assembly was at Loughborough. The locomotive was equipped by Brush with a Petter SS4 360 bhp two-stroke oil engine, and Brush 190 kW generator with continuous rating at 600 rpm. Two traction motors were fitted, each one driving an outer axle through double reduction gearing. Its outward general appearance made the locomotive similar to the LMS twin motor design, then in production, but followed the LNER examples more closely. Because 15004 was air-started there were no large battery boxes mounted on the running board, although the generator had a starting field, and an empty conduit spanned the engine room under the sump. These provisions were made so that a battery starter could be fitted, but in fact one never was. It appeared in grey livery with no markings, and undertook some shunting in the LMS yard at Loughborough. Trials took place on the Eastern region at Stratford (Temple Mills) and March during 1948 and in early 1949 it again undertook a day's shunting in Loughborough yard, for the benefit of some Siamese visitors.

In 1949, after successful trials, the locomotive was accepted into British Railways stock and allocated the number 15004, no Brush works number being allocated at any time. During 1955, 15004 was shedded at Hornsey, and from time to time spent periods at Derby works; its final allocation was New England, from where it was withdrawn in October 1962, being cut up at Doncaster works soon afterwards.

Another similar locomotive was added to British Railways stock in November 1949, but this was built at the Swindon works of the former Great Western Railway. This locomotive was originally allocated the number 501 under the Great Western 1946 renumbering scheme, but since delivery was later than intended, it finally appeared as 15107, being produced as Swindon Lot 363. It was identical in outline to the English Electric – LMS 0–6–0s, and was fitted with a Petter 360 bhp diesel engine and Brush equipment similar to that used in 15004, but had a battery starter. The locomotive weighed 46.1 tons and had a tractive effort of 33,500 lb, whereas 15004 was 51.4 tons with 32,000 lb tractive effort. Number 15107 appeared in standard British Railways black livery with the characteristic Swindon numberplates and was set to work at Bristol, where indeed it ended its working days (at Bristol St. Philips Marsh), being withdrawn from service in June 1958 after a comparatively short life. It was later cut up at Swindon works. These first two locomotives were reasonably successful in themselves, but as with most single examples were non-standard and destined for short lives in any case. No repeat orders ensued from British Railways, but at least orders from industry for similar locomotives did develop later, proving that there was an alternative to the English Electric 0–6–0 Diesel.

8. The first Brush 0-6-0 diesel-electric shunter, seen in November 1947, on the southern exchange sidings at Falcon Works. During 1949 it was taken into British Railways (Eastern Region) stock, and numbered 15004. Brush Electrical Machines.

9. During December 1948 15004 returned to Loughborough and is seen shunting in the British Railways goods yard there. Siamese visitors were given a demonstration of its capabilities when it replaced the customary steam locomotive for the day. B.E.M.

10. Although Brush supplied the traction equipment for BR 15107, it was built at Swindon in 1949 and carried a Great Western type brass cabside numberplate. As a non-standard design it only had a short working life, being withdrawn and scrapped in 1958.

Early in 1948 the first of five more Brush-equipped 0–6–0 diesels entered service in Eire. During the Second World War Eire, although neutral, had experienced difficulties in obtaining coal from Britain for her steam locomotives and a pilot scheme for diesel locomotives was initiated by the C.I.E. Chairman, Mr. A. P. Reynolds. Brush received the order for the design and supply of equipment through Associated Locomotive Equipment Ltd., an organisation in which the Deputy Chairman and Managing Director, Mr. Good, was involved and the order was placed early in 1945. The five diesels were intended for shunting and transfer duties in and around Dublin. Inchicore works commenced building in May 1947, the first, No. 1000, being completed by December of that year, and the remainder, 1001–4, during 1948.

The diesel engine fitted was a Mirrlees industrial TLDT6 vertical six-cylinder direct-injection four stroke turbo-pressure-charge type with 8½in bore and 13¾in stroke, developing 487 bhp at 710 rpm continuous rating, and 535 bhp at one hour rating. Directly coupled to it was a Brush 290 kW d.c. generator with a top-mounted 10 kW auxiliary generator, multi-belt driven from a pulley on the main generator shaft. Nose suspended traction motors were fitted on the outer axles, each having a continuous rated output of 177 bhp at 1200 volts.

The overall length was 29ft with an 11ft 9in wheelbase; total weight in full working order was 52 tons 19cwt. No. 1000 entered service in January 1948 and it soon became apparent, initial snags apart, that the new units would be very satisfactory.

The service on which 1000–4 were to be engaged was transfer rail to sea traffic between Kingsbridge (Heuston since 1966) and North Wall yards, six miles of steeply graded line, which included 1½ miles of 1 in 84. Load requirements here were thirty-five wagons of 400 ton gross maximum to be hauled at speeds up to 25 mph. At lower speeds, fifty wagons totalling 600 tons gross could be hauled in the yards. Tests also proved that even starting 400 ton loads on the steepest gradient, with greasy rail and adverse weather conditions, the locomotives had an ample margin with the power equipment operating within its continuous rating.

An unusual test was conducted on 21 March 1948 when 1000 hauled a 350 ton train non-stop from Dublin to Cork, a journey of 165 miles in 8 hours 40 minutes. At that time steam locomotives required 11 hours 50 minutes for the same journey. The really outstanding achievement was that the locomotive successfully undertook the task of continuous main line work, a duty for which it had not been designed. Additionally a fuel cost saving of 75 per cent was achieved over steam haulage on the same route.

Once the locomotives settled down to their intended duties they could be seen at North Wall, shunting empty stock at Kingsbridge, or shunting around Inchicore. In the mid-fifties they were renumbered D301–5 and all but No. 302 (withdrawn 1966) were phased out of use by early 1973. No Brush works numbers were ever allocated to these locomotives.

11. Coras Iompair Eireann No. 1000 (later D 301) as running in 1948. Although not actually built by Brush this locomotive and its four sisters had Brush electrical equipment and paved the way for the Brush-Bagnall industrial shunters.   B.E.M.

12. The first to be withdrawn was D 302 (formerly 1001) in 1966. It is seen here at Inchicore awaiting disposal along with other discarded equipment.   H. Richards, I.R.R.S.

THE BRUSH – BAGNALL ERA

As already demonstrated the dynamic character of Mr. A. P. Good had enabled experience to be gained with 0–6–0 diesel-electric shunters through his interests in Associated Locomotive Equipment Ltd., which was a subsidiary of Heenan & Froude Ltd. Since 1938 it had been Mr. Good's intention to dominate the oil engine industry and he used his professional skill as a solicitor to gain control of companies despite attempts to evade this by some of them. His sound business mind, combined with financial backing, grouped together a number of companies, in which he was the key link, into associated but individual groups.

His next move was to acquire, on behalf of Heenan & Froude Ltd., W. G. Bagnall Ltd. of Stafford, the old established firm of locomotive engineers. The death in 1947 of Mr. W. S. Edwards, Bagnall's Managing Director and effectively, sole shareholder, had led to the holding being offered for sale. A. P. Good acquired Bagnalls, thereby securing an established locomotive works. At the same time he proposed the 1948 oil engine merger of Brush, Petters Ltd. (already Brush controlled), with Mirrlees Bickerton & Day Ltd., J. & H. McLaren Ltd. and Oil Engines (Coventry) Ltd. The result was the Brush, Associated British Oil Engine Group. Overall it was now possible to go ahead with diesel-electric production and seek orders because, with a common Chairman, single control over engines, electrical mechanical parts and final locomotive erection had been gained.

Ten stock diesel-electric shunters were authorised (Brush-Bagnall 2971–6, 3000–3) Brush being the main contractor. At the same time provision was made for their construction at Stafford, but under Brush engineers' supervision. Although the previous seven 0–6–0 diesel-electrics had been ordered for ordinary railway use, and were partial off-shoots of the already established English Electric concept, the future trend was towards industrial use. The frames for the new 0–6–0 locomotives were laid during 1950, four being destined for the Steel Company of Wales' Port Talbot Works, and numbered 701–4, with works Nos. 3000–3 respectively.

At the same time three ultra-modern 0–6–0 saddle tank steam locomotives were built for the Steel Company by Bagnalls, for comparative trials with the new diesels.

The new diesels were rated at 480 bhp being fitted with Mirrlees TLS6 engines. Externally they followed previous practice, but had plain flat asbestos-lined protective bonnet fronts enclosing the radiators, to counteract the effect of excessive heat within the steelworks when employed on ladle duties. Heavier frames and

13. The initial product of the Brush-Bagnall association was a stock batch of 0-6-0 diesel-electric shunters. The first four of them went to the Steel Company of Wales' Port Talbot works. Brush-Bagnall 3000 (S.C.O.W. 701) is seen here at Bagnall's works in undercoat finish. B.E.M.

14. The last member of the batch, Steel Company of Wales No. 704 (B-B 3003), resplendent in maroon livery and wasp-stripes, at Port Talbot works. Note the plain bonnet front and deep buffer beams. This locomotive was scrapped in 1974.
British Steel Corporation.

15. A later example of the stock batch (B-B 2973) became Steel Company of Wales No. 711. Note the normal radiator arrangement with steel protective plate and lowered cab roof.
British Steel Corporation.

deeper buffer beams were additional features affording better protection and safety within the industrial confines. Yellow and black wasp stripes were later applied liberally by the Steel Company to aid better visibility. Main dimensions were:

Length over Buffers	29ft 8in
Total Wheelbase	11ft 6in
Wheel Diameter	4ft 0in
Weight in Working Order	55 tons
Maximum Starting Tractive Effort	32,000 lb
Maximum Speed	20 mph

Delivery took place in April 1951 and in the form of locomotives all four spent their entire lives at Abbey Works until 1970, working under extremely arduous conditions. Loads during the early period were usually ingots and molten metal ladles, but when such loads subsequently became too heavy they were relegated to yard duties and interchange siding duties. Three of them, 702–4, were scrapped in 1974, but 701 underwent a curious conversion, into what was termed a "braked runner" after its withdrawal. The British Steel Corporation (Steel Company of Wales' successor) removed the power unit, superstructure, traction motors and the centre pair of driving wheels. They then added a box filled with 28 tons of concrete above footplate level and installed automatic air braking which could be controlled by the propelling locomotive. The overall weight of the four-wheeler was 50 tons, and its purpose was to provide locomotives with additional braking power when handling heavy trains on steep gradients.

At some time number 703 lost its side rods and ran as a six-wheeled diesel-electric.

In January 1950 another order for an 0–6–0 diesel-electric locomotive was received from Lever Brothers Ltd., Port Sunlight. This order was for a virtually identical design to the Welsh units, except for standard frames. It, too, was built at Stafford and may have been the very first Brush-Bagnall to emerge, carrying works No. 2971 (one of the intended stock locomotives sold prior to completion); delivery was early in 1951. No running number was allotted, but the name *Montgomery of Alamein* was painted on the side battery box covers, in shaded block letters. This locomotive was out of use from 1959 to 1967 and was stored off its wheels until sold to Stanley Davies Plant Hire of Middlesex in March 1967, soon afterwards arriving on a low loader at Falcon Works, for repair. With one traction motor removed and some rewiring undertaken 2971 was used on railway dismantling duties in Central Wales during 1968, but by 1970 the locomotive had returned to Middlesex, where is was scrapped.

16. Brush-Bagnall 2971 was supplied to Lever Brothers Ltd. in 1951 for use at their Port Sunlight works. No running number was allotted, but in keeping with Lever's normal practice of naming its engines after national figures, this one was named *Montgomery of Alamein*.
B.E.M.

The Consett Iron Company also placed an order with Brush during January 1950 for two more basically similar 0–6–0 diesel shunters. These also were built at Stafford, as Brush-Bagnall 3020–1 (running numbers 5 and 6) and delivered in March 1952 and May 1952 respectively. They were fitted with Mirrlees TL6 355 bhp engines and each locomotive weighed 56 tons in full working order. The pair worked at the Consett Works until September 1969, when No. 5 was scrapped on site; number 6 was sold to the British Steel Corporation's Trostre Works, South Wales, in August 1971, being transported there by road soon afterwards. It is still at Trostre, where it is used as standby locomotive. Two of the Brush-Bagnall locomotives, 2975–6, were cancelled but some of the parts already manufactured were probably incorporated in 3020–1.

In 1952 two more orders were received for 0–6–0 shunters, the first in January, for the Steel Company of Wales' Trostre Works, and the second in December, for its Abbey Works. The earlier order, for one locomotive, was met by 2972, of the original stock batch, and it was delivered from Stafford during mid-1952, being allocated running number 1 at Trostre. It was generally similar to the basic Brush-Bagnall 355 bhp 0–6–0 locomotives delivered previously to industry. During 1957 it was transferred to the Abbey Works and renumbered 713, continuing to work there until 1974, when it was observed intact but out of use. Some years previously it had been converted to four-wheel drive.

The latter order, which was for two 350 bhp locomotives of the same basic design, was also met from the stock batch, for quick delivery, only minor alterations being needed to suit Steel Company requirements. The two were completed in April 1953, as works numbers 2973–4 (Abbey Works 711–2) and delivered soon afterwards. One detail difference which was quite noticeable

was the reversion to exposed front radiator grille and the exclusion of protective bonnet doors. Number 712 was transferred from Abbey Works to Velindre in 1959, but underwent a modification which converted it into an 0–4–0. The centre pair of wheels were removed thus reducing the unladen weight to 51 tons and enabling the locomotive to negotiate the curves at Velindre, which were of generally smaller radius than those at Abbey. By April 1976 it had become the reserve locomotive.

Number 711 remained at Abbey Works for many years, working alongside 701–4 and 713, initially employed on ingot and hot metal duties, but latterly in the yards, until it was withdrawn from service in 1970. Like 701, mentioned previously, it was converted into a braked runner and still survives in this condition. In all, between 1951 and 1970 the six locomotives accumulated a total of 385,035 hours worked, a very creditable record.

17. A typical Brush-Bagnall brass worksplate. This one was fitted to Steel Company of Wales No. 713 (Abbey Works). Notice that only Loughborough appears on the plate although the locomotive was actually constructed at Stafford.

18. Another of the original stock batch was Brush-Bagnall 2972, which was supplied new in 1952 to the Steel Company of Wales' Trostre Works, where it became No. 1, as seen here in July 1955. Later it was transferred to Abbey Works, where it was renumbered 713.   B.E.M.

19. The earliest main-line locomotives built by Brush were twenty-five A1A-A1As for the Ceylon Government Railways. The first was No. 539 (B-B 3025) seen here on the Brush test track in 1952, prior to delivery. B.E.M.

The year 1950 brought a new development to the Brush-Bagnall association in the form of an order for 25 1000 bhp A1A-A1A main line diesel locomotives for the Ceylon Government Railways. This came about as a direct result of the Technical Director's visit to North America two years previously in which he studied the development and usage of diesel-electric traction. The findings of his visit were most encouraging and resulted in the Company deciding to compete for the main line market. This policy was successful, for the £1,000,000 order placed through the Crown Agents for the Colonies was won virtually straight from the drawing board, and gained in the face of competition from other companies with previous experience in the field.

Mr. B. D. Rampala, Chief Mechanical Engineer of Ceylon Government Railways, had visited Britain to select a suitable type of unit, which the railway required. Discussions on final design were held between himself, the Crown Agents and Brush, which resulted in the order finally being placed on 13 March 1950. Indeed as there were only two main line diesel-electric locomotives in regular service in Britain at that time (the LMS-English Electric 10000 and 10001) and British Railways was still committed to steam, the order was something to be proud of. With the importance of the contract and the arduous operating conditions in Ceylon it was decided that two engineers would be sent there to evaluate the railway system in detail. Gradients as steep as 1 in 40, altitudes of 6000 ft, short radius curves and humid, saline tropical conditions all had to be provided for in the design. Meanwhile at the Falcon Works new workshop facilities were being erected to allow an annual production rate of 36 main line diesel-electrics. In addition, a new test track, test house and extensions to the internal railway system were speedily

installed and by October 1952 the first Ceylon locomotive was complete. It was Brush-Bagnall 3025 and Ceylon Government Railways 539, being designated Class M1; the remainder of the class was consecutively numbered up to 3049, and Ceylon 563.

Although the locomotives were erected at Loughborough, the underframes and mechanical parts were manufactured at Stafford and the Mirrlees engines which powered them were produced at Stockport. The locomotives were fitted with a V-type 12-cylinder, turbo-charged, four-stroke diesel engine with a normal-condition rating of 1250 bhp at 850 rpm, but rated in Ceylon at 1000 bhp at 850 rpm. Its previous application had been as a marine engine. Directly coupled to it was a Brush d.c. main generator of 652 kW, 630/750v 1035/870 amps continuous rating. Four Brush traction motors were fitted, being of the nose-suspended type of 196 bhp continuous rating, 226 bhp one hour rating. Air braking equipment was supplied by Westinghouse Brake & Signal Company Ltd. The weight of each locomotive was 87 tons in full working order; other details were as follows:

Track Gauge	5ft 6in
Length over Buffers	50ft 9in
Maximum Height	13ft 3½in
Maximum Width	10ft 3⅞in
Bogie Wheelbase	10ft 6in
Bogie Centres	27ft 0in
Minimum Curve Radius	5 chains
Fuel Capacity (Main)	775 gallons
Fuel Capacity (Service)	75 gallons

Locomotives all fitted for Multiple-Working.

The exterior appearance was more functional than elegant, but during the early 1950s the attention to clean and uncluttered exterior lines was not generally considered to be essential. Certainly they looked impressive, with a short nose at each end and two widely spaced front windows above, but forward vision must have been restricted. 'Porthole' windows, heavy wire mesh grilles and three sets of louvres were set in the body sides, and in contrast the running numbers were set centrally in raised metal, as was a long waist line reaching horizontally from cab to cab, almost in 10,000/10,001 style. The works plates were affixed below the numerals. The roof was divided into three sections which were removable for heavy repair needs, but incorporating top hatches for engine maintenance access.

Delivery of the locomotives from the works was by road on low-loaders, or by rail on special adaptor bogies which had been made for them. They were dispatched from Loughborough between early 1953 and October 1955.

An official handing-over ceremony was held at Falcon Works, but 539 did not take part as intended because it had to be dispatched to Birkenhead in time for loading on board the S.S. *Clan McQueen*. Instead 540 was used, and it was officially handed over to the High Commissioner of Ceylon by Sir Ronald Matthews on 20 November 1952.

The Brush-Bagnall association had been developed by Mr. A. P. Good into a selling company by February 1951 and was called Brush-Bagnall Traction Ltd. W. G. Bagnall Ltd. continued to exist as a separate organisation and was never absorbed into the Associated Brush Oil Engine group. The firm also continued to build steam and diesel-mechanical locomotives on its own account concurrently with the diesel-electrics.

The future policy of Brush-Bagnall Traction was to co-ordinate the diesel-electric activities of Mirrlees, Brush and Bagnalls, with the latter building the shunters and Loughborough the main line locomotives. Mr. Good toured the U.S.A. and Commonwealth countries, but an expected order from the Queensland Government Railways for a Mirrlees J12 engined locomotive never materialised. The works number 3057 allotted to it was cancelled. Later in 1951 the National Gas & Oil Engine Company Ltd. came completely into Mr. Good's control through Brush. A new erecting shop was authorised at Stafford and was completed by 1953, in time to take on work for the Ceylon locomotives.

All through the period 1951 to 1956 the works numbers of Brush-Bagnall locomotives were allocated from within the existing Bagnall list, but of course the new title appeared on the works plates in place of the previous one. Tragically Mr. Good died early in 1953 and at once the effective connection between Bagnall and Brush was severed. Heenan & Froude Ltd. owned Bagnalls, and it was their disinterest in locomotive affairs which led to a cooling in relations and eventual parting as a selling company.

20. The fourth of the Ceylon locomotives, No. 542 (B-B 3028) ready for dispatch by rail to Birkenhead in January 1953. Notice the special bogies fitted for rail delivery in Britain and *Ace*, the then works shunter, formerly at the Yeovil works of Petters Ltd.
B.E.M.

21. Another view of the same locomotive marshalled in a goods train as it was about to set out for Birkenhead in February 1953. This siding to the rear of Loughborough Midland station witnessed many similar departures in the years up to 1968. B.E.M.

During April 1953 further industrial locomotive orders were received, not only for 0–6–0s, but also 0–4–0s and Bo-Bos too. These orders represented three of the four basic designs offered by Brush-Bagnall for general railway and industrial use during that period. The fourth design, for a centre-cab Bo-Bo rated at 750 bhp, never materialised. The intended range offered was as follows:

0–4–0	with 375bhp M4 AAU6	National engine	Supercharged
0–6–0	with 400bhp or 540bhp	National normal R4 AA6 engine Mirrlees normal J6 engine	
Bo-Bo	with 540bhp or 750bhp	Mirrlees normal J6 engine Mirrlees Supercharged JS6 engine	
Bo-Bo	Centre cab with two 375bhp M4 AU6 engines	National Supercharged	

The 0–6–0 order, which came from the National Coal Board in South Wales, was for two 400 bhp shunters to be used at Cwm Colliery. These two locomotives were Brush-Bagnall 3073/4 and received N.C.B. numbers 1 and 2 respectively. They were built at Stafford and delivery took place in September 1955. The basic design was as before, but some differences began to emerge, such as a considerably lowered roof section immediately in front of the cab, to give better cross vision for drivers when running forward. This limited forward vision had always been an undesirable operating feature of all shunters with end cabs and high power unit compartments. An additional centrally-placed front cab window was fitted to aid vision. The engine specified was the National Gas & Oil Engine Company type R4AA6, a four-stroke six-cylinder design developing 400 bhp at 750 rpm instead of the Mirrlees type formerly used. These two locomotives were still at Cwm early in 1976 working on the exchange sidings.

22. Brush-Bagnall 3074 was the second of two units ordered by the National Coal Board for use at Cwm Colliery in South Wales, where it was No. 2. It is seen standing outside the Bagnall works at Stafford in 1955. The cut-down superstructure in front of the cab, to aid the driver's cross-vision, is strikingly different from all previous designs.
B.E.M.

23. One of a pair of Brush-Bagnall 0-6-0s (B-B 3094/5) supplied to Stewart & Lloyds in 1955/6 for their Corby steelworks. They worked there until scrapped about 1972. B.E.M.

24. An artist's impression of the proposed Brush-Bagnall twin-engine Bo-Bo design of 1953. It was intended to equip them with 375 b.h.p. National engines. B.E.M.

The new 0–4–0 design appeared with a batch of seven sturdy and attractively styled machines ordered by the Steel Company of Wales Ltd. They were built at Stafford Works (works numbers 3066–72, running, numbers 501–7) and delivered to the Abbey Works, between December 1954 and June 1955. The order was the result of the Steel Company's policy of expansion, which included the standardisation of the Brush-Bagnall 300 bhp 0–4–0 for lighter and general steel-works duties, as well as the 500 bhp bogie design for heavier duties. The latter cost more to build, but the resultant service savings more than offset this by reduced wheel wear on the severe track curvature encountered at the steel works.

Once in service the 0–4–0s became very popular with their respective users. The batch was fitted with National M4AAU6, 6-cylinder engines, which developed 300 bhp at 1200 rpm and onto which was directly coupled a Brush d.c. main generator, mounted on a common bed plate. This generator supplied power to two double-reduction geared, nose-suspended traction motors. As all clearances in the works were generous, to accommodate the American Locomotive Company locomotives, the opportunity was taken to fit a generously-proportioned cab to these 0–4–0 locomotives. Main details were as follows:

Rigid Wheelbase	8ft 0in
Length over Buffers	25ft 5½in
Overall Height	13ft 2¾in
Maximum Width	9ft 8in
Wheel Diameter	3ft 6in
Minimum Curve Negotiable	80ft radius
Weight in Working Order	43 tons 5 cwt
Fuel Capacity	275 gallons
Maximum Speed	20 mph
Maximum Tractive Effort	24,000 lb

25. The first examples of the new 0-4-0 design were an order for seven to be supplied to the Steel Company of Wales' Abbey Works, where they were Nos. 501-7 (B-B 3066-72). They worked there as single units until 1971/2 when they were converted for working in tandem.
B.E.M.

The cab arrangement was very good, with a centrally-placed rear access door and excellent all round vision, as a result of the numerous windows, the side windows being of the horizontally sliding type. An additional door in the front of the cab gave access to the railed-in footplate, which was provided around the sides and front of the power compartment. The fuel tank was situated below the cab floor.

26. Another standard 0-4-0, Brush-Bagnall 3096, seen on the Falcon Works track, with the Great Central main-line in the background. The works plate was moved to a lower position before delivery.
B.E.M.

On this batch of locomotives the front bonnet was plain, the radiator air louvres being on the bonnet top and sides. Large circular buffers were mounted on deep heavy buffer beams, which in turn were welded to the equally robust plate frames and deck. Straight air braking was provided, operating on all wheels, with one brake shoe per wheel acting upon the inner side of the wheel. In addition, a handbrake located inside the cab acted upon all wheels. The single-stage twin-cylinder air compressor was belt driven from the engine. Radio telephone equipment was mounted inside the cab between the two front windows.

All these locomotives remain in service at the Abbey Works, but after the 0–6–0 diesel shunters there had been phased out some of the batch were converted for working in tandem during 1971/2. They were dealt with as follows: 501 'master' and 502 'slave'. They were also used in conjunction with later units supplied and similarly dealt with at the same time. Incidentally 503/6/7 have been re-engined by the British Steel Corporation with 335 bhp Rolls Royce engines.

27. A Loughborough-built 0-4-0 of 1956 (B-B 3097), seen in March 1976 at the Velindre Works of the British Steel Corporation, where it was numbered LD1.   British Steel Corporation.

28. Margam & Abbey Works 509 (Master) and 502 (Slave) working in tandem. Notice that the slave unit has had its cab removed.
British Steel Corporation.

29. Another of the 1956 Loughborough-built Brush-Bagnall 0-4-0s (B-B 3098) hard at work in the Abbey Works. This was the first of the second batch of 0-4-0s (508-11) supplied to Abbey Works.
British Steel Corporation.

The new Bo-Bo order received was also for the Steel Company of Wales' Abbey Works which preferred Bo-Bo types after their experience with the 1950 American examples, which gave such good performance. These impressive machines emerged from Loughborough between March and June 1955. They were Brush-Bagnall 3063/4/5 and were numbered 901/2/3. Very impressive lines graced these 515 bhp shunters and they bore a very obvious family resemblance to the 0–6–0 and 0–4–0 shunters, with their bonnet and radiator design, lowered rear power compartment roof profile and excellent cab, as fitted to the 0–4–0s. One very striking feature was the bold wasp-stripe warning panels covering extensive areas, very easily noticed. These locomotives were heralded as the most powerful industrial shunters in Great Britain, which indeed they were at the time of introduction. Main details were:

Maximum Tractive Effort	47,000 lb
Bogie Wheelbase	8ft 0in
Bogie Centres	18ft 6in
Length over Buffers	38ft 5½in
Overall Height	13ft 3in
Overall Width	9ft 8in
Wheel Diameter	3ft 6in
Minimum Curve Negotiable	80ft radius (running light) 150ft radius (loaded)
Weight in Working Order	70 tons
Fuel Capacity	350 gallons
Maximum Speed	28 mph

The diesel engine was supplied by Mirrlees, a 6-cylinder, four-stroke type J6, developing 515 bhp at 875 rpm. Directly coupled to it was the Brush d.c. main generator of the self-ventilated, compound-wound type. A small bonnet to the rear of the cab housed blower equipment and ducting for the force ventilated traction motors on the rear bogie. The bogies were of fabricated steel plate construction, with the main frames lying on the coil spring suspension. Clasp type air brakes were fitted, with double acting cylinders. As with the 0–4–0s radio telephone equipment was mounted centrally between the front windows, inside the cab. These three locomotives were still in use at Abbey Works in early 1977.

33. A later shot of the same locomotive, now in working livery and numbered 902, seen moving one of the special molten steel containers at Abbey Works.　　　British Steel Corporation.

In March 1956 two 0–6–0 diesel shunters were supplied from Loughborough to Stewarts & Lloyds steelworks at Corby, Northamptonshire, from an order placed in late 1953. Again these followed the pattern of low roof profile ahead of the cab. Mirrlees 6-cylinder engines of 366 bhp were installed and these machines worked at Corby until scrapped about 1972. They were Brush-Bagnall 3094–5 and numbered D6 and D7 respectively. D6 had, incidentally, been on demonstration prior to sale.

Also in March 1956 Loughborough completed two more 0–4–0s for the Steel Company of Wales, Brush-Bagnall 3096–7. The former was Trostre Works number 1 and the latter Velindre Works LD1. Trostre 1 was later re-numbered 3, and has been used mainly on shunting loads of steel coils from British Railways sidings to the works, and returning with loaded 'Shocvans' each carrying two tons of bulk tinplate. The locomotive has to be available on a 24-hour basis but the Brush-Bagnall 3021 is its standby during maintenance periods. It is expected to be in service till about 1986. The Velindre locomotive (3097) still works there on normal shunting duties and, in common with other British Steel Corporation locomotives, still has conspicuous wasp stripes. Both locomotives were equipped with National 6-cylinder four-stroke type M4 AAU6 engines, rated at 300 bhp.

During 1955 more industrial orders were received for 0–4–0 and Bo-Bos totalling £240,000. The first, placed in June 1955, was for six 0–4–0 shunters of 300 bhp, once more using the National M4 AAU6. Again they were destined for the Steel Company of Wales' Abbey Works, which numbered them from 508–13 (Brush-Bagnall 3098–3103) and were delivered by road from Loughborough during 1956. A second order, of one more identical unit (B-B 3120) for Abbey Works, was placed in November 1955. This was numbered 514 and delivered in 1957. These seven locomotives worked with the previous batch at Abbey Works until 1971/2 when they were converted to multiple working, and 510 was re-engined with a Rolls Royce engine; 508–11 became 'master' units and 512–14 'slaves', with their cabs removed. All are still in service there.

The Bo-Bo order was placed by the Steel Company of Wales in August 1955, for the Abbey Works but this time it was for three enlarged output version of 88½ tons, each rated at 660 bhp. Again Loughborough erected them and delivery took place in 1957. They were Brush-Bagnall 3111–3 and bore Steel Company numbers 951–3 respectively. The engine fitted was a Mirrlees JS6 type four-stroke 6-cylinder, developing 660 bhp at 875 rpm or 600 bhp at 850 rpm. Drop bar equalising beams were fitted to the bogies of these heavier locomotives. It is a matter of interest to note that these locomotives were among the last official Brush-Bagnall locomotives to be produced under that title and the 0–4–0 3120 was the highest joint locomotive number within the works list. The decline after 1953 in the Bagnall interest had made Brush decide to enlarge its own mechanical engineering department to cover this aspect and 1956 saw the new organisation emerge as Brush Traction Ltd. W. G. Bagnall and Brush Traction went their separate ways, but co-operated closely for a period afterwards, mainly on underframes and mechanical parts.

34. The last of the ten Bo-Bo shunters supplied to the Steel Company of Wales, pulling wagons of ingot moulds within the steelworks on 9 May 1962.   B.E.M.

THE BRUSH TRACTION ERA OF THE TYPE 2s

The new organisation's emergence coincided with another important event which completely changed the situation at Loughborough. This was British Railways' 1955 modernisation scheme, in which it was planned to replace steam locomotives eventually by diesels and electrics. It had been decided to initiate a diesel pilot scheme involving 171 (later 174) locomotives for main line use and speedy delivery was an essential factor of the programme. Although there had been seven main-line diesels in existence for several years on British Railways, sufficiently widespread experience was lacking, so it was emphasised at the time that these new diesels would not necessarily be the future standard types.

Brush Traction's previous experience of large diesel-electric locomotives led to an order being placed by the British Transport Commission in November 1955 for twenty 1250 bhp A1A-A1A 'Ceylon' type locomotives, suitable for British use. The initial artist's impressions developed the Ceylon outline slightly by removing the nose sections and substituting a flat cab front reaching downwards to combine with the buffer beam and extending nearly to track level. This was an approach towards clean lines, but above the intended inter-locomotive connection door two very uninspiring windows were placed. The side panels retained three porthole windows and some cleaned-up louvres, but overall the design was of fairly depressing appearance. Fortunately, as things progressed, the British Transport Commission design consultants modified it to the now familiar outlines which vary only in detail. At one stage in 1957 a wooden mock-up cab was produced bearing these familiar lines and the number D505.

35. A first projection drawing of how the Ceylon design was to be adapted to the Type 2 concept. Notice the gangway front end.
B.E.M.

36. Once a decision had been reached about the general external form of the Type 2, a wooden mock-up cab was made in November 1956, for evaluation purposes. Why the number D 505 was chosen is not known, but it was given a more relevant one when exhibited in 1958.
B.E.M.

37. An artist's revised impression of the Brush Type 2 before the British Transport Commission Design Panel re-styled it. This re-styling undoubtedly enhanced the locomotive's appearance and paved the way for the now familiar outline of the Type 4. B.E.M.

By mid-1957 construction of the new Type 2 locomotives was well under way and the first one was scheduled to be completed within two years of the order being placed. It was finished five weeks ahead of schedule and undertook its first run in workshop brown livery, bearing British Railways' new lion and wheel emblem and the number D5500. The twenty locomotives ordered were D5500–19, Brush Traction 71–90. The underframes of D5515–19 were made at Stafford and allocated Bagnall numbers 3127–31.

The lowest Brush Traction number issued was 71 and was derived in theory by being the sum total Brush and Brush-Bagnall production plus one. Strangely this did not include the 1940 *Sprite* conversion, but did include others not built under the Brush-Bagnall association and also some stock cancellations. Main details of D5500–19 were:

Engine (JVS12T)	Mirrlees V-type 12-cylinder, turbo charged, four-stroke. 1250 bhp at 850 rpm.
Main Generator	823 kW 686 volts 1200 amps 820 kW 820 volts 1000 amps
Traction Motors (4)	250 bhp 343 volts 600 amps 485 rpm. Continuous rating. Force ventilated, nose-suspended axle-hung.

Locomotive		
	Weight	104 tons
	Height	12ft 7in
	Width	8ft 9in
	Length Overall	56ft 9in
	Bogie Wheelbase	14ft 0in
	Bogie Centres	28ft 10in
	Minimum Curve	4½ chains
	Fuel Capacity	500 gallons
	Maximum Speed	75 mph
	Maximum Tractive Effort	42,000 lb
	Continuous Tractive Effort	22,400 lb

'Commonwealth' one piece cast steel bogies.

38. The first Type 2, D 5500, begins to take shape in the erecting shop at Falcon Works in 1957. The frame of another unit can be seen at the far right.   B.E.M.

Westinghouse brake equipment was fitted, with vacuum for the train and compressed air for the locomotive. The locomotive brakes were applied automatically via the vacuum equipment and also by the independent brake valve.

The first Brush Type 2 was completed during the last week in September 1957 and appeared in undercoat finish for running its initial trials to Chinley, on the Midland main-line in Derbyshire, prior to being prepared for the handing over ceremony. The final livery was British Railways Brunswick green, with two horizontal grey-white lines running completely around the locomotive, one below cab window level and one at deck level. The cab window area, both front and sides, was picked out in white, a feature unique to D5500–19; all the roof sections were grey. The running numbers of most of the batch appeared once on each side and the heraldic lion and wheel emblem was the newer version, then recently introduced.

The handing over ceremony was held on Thursday 31 October 1957 and attended by the press and dignitaries of Brush, the British Transport Commission and British Railways Eastern Region. Sir Reginald Wilson accepted D5500 on behalf of British Railways Eastern Region from Mr. Geoffrey Eley, Chairman of the Brush Group of Companies. Also present were Mr. R. C. Bond (British Railways Chief Mechanical Engineer) Mr. Maurice Tattersfield (Brush Loughborough Managing Director) and Mr. F. H. Wood, then Manager of Brush Traction. Much was made of this occasion, quite rightly too, with demonstration runs up and down the test track.

39. The first Brush Type 2 (D 5500; Brush Traction 71) nearing completion at Loughborough in the late summer of 1957. The second and third are well advanced, while the frames of a fourth can be seen on the right. Notice the gangway connection fitted to all the Type 2s, but rarely used in service. In winter they were the cause of unwelcome draughts and some were permanently sealed.
B.E.M.

40. The revised cab design, as seen on one of the initial batch of twenty, D 5515 (Brush Traction 85).
B.E.M.

41. D 5500 standing at Chinley station, on the occasion of its first trial run, 10 October 1957. B.E.M.

42. Another works view, early in 1959, showing D 5537 of the second batch being lowered onto its bogies. The board on the buffer housing was a constant reminder to all concerned of the target date for completion. B.E.M.

BRITISH RAILWAYS
40 TYPE B LOCOMOTIVES
No. 18
CONTRACT Nº 04/45800
Target Date for Test June 4th 1959

Facing page
43. D 5531 (Brush Traction 130) of the second batch poses on the test track prior to delivery in May 1959. Compare this shot with D 5515 on page 26 for the difference in appearance caused by changing to roller blinds for the route indicator and the revised style of letter D for the running number. B.E.M.

Normally Thursday was the day when locomotives left Loughborough for their acceptance trials. A British Railways crew would take over the locomotive, with Brush engineers in attendance, and drive it to the Chief Mechanical & Electrical Engineer's department at Doncaster, where it was thoroughly checked and tested.

Road tests would follow, a passenger train to and from Peterborough and a 750 ton freight train to and from Spalding. Within a week Brush would receive the acceptance certificate and the locomotive would enter regular revenue earning service, which in 1958 was on the Great Eastern lines out of London to East Anglia. D5500 initially went to Stratford motive power depot. Deliveries were as follows: 1957 D5500–2 and 1958 D5503–19, at approximately two locomotives a month. D5501 went on exhibition, prior to delivery, at Mirrlees' Hazel Grove Works, Stockport, as part of the celebrations commemorating fifty years of diesel engine production there. Meanwhile, on 13 November 1957, D5500 hauled its first revenue earning train, the 10.36 Liverpool Street to Clacton, on the Great Eastern lines. D5500–19 were classified D12/12 by the Eastern Region.

44. One of the new works shunters, built by Beyer-Peacock, pushes an almost-complete Type 2 into the test house in 1960. B.E.M.

While the British Railways Type 2 designs were in preparation Brush constructed seven more 515 bhp Bo-Bo shunters to the order of the Steel Company of Wales, again for their Abbey Works. The underframes were constructed at Stafford and were allocated Bagnall numbers 3137–43. In addition they had Brush Traction numbers, 92–98, and running numbers 904–910 respectively. Ordered in 1956, delivery took place from Stafford in 1957/58 as Brush were by now engaged on Type 2 construction.

The first post Brush-Bagnall 0–4–0 shunter was ordered by the Steel Company of Wales in July 1956, for their Orb Works near Newport. Noticeable visual changes from previous 0–4–0s were the front radiator grille, modified cab with more curved contours, a lack of footplate handrails, and three side bonnet grilles.

A National 220 bhp engine was fitted and other details were as follows:

Wheelbase	6ft 0in
Driving Wheel Diameter	3ft 6in
Minimum Curve	60ft radius
Weight in Working Order	30 tons
Fuel Capacity	200 gallons
Single Traction Motor	160 bhp for 1 hour
Maximum Tractive Effort	19,200 lb
Maximum Speed	18 mph

This particular locomotive was built at Beyer-Peacock's Gorton Works, Manchester in 1957/58, the first of several orders for this type. Two works numbers were allotted, Beyer-Peacock 7856 and Brush Traction 91, of which only the latter appeared on the oval works plate; no running number was allocated by the Steel Company. It was placed in service at Orb Works in September 1958, where it is still employed on general shunting duties.

45. The first Brush/Beyer-Peacock 0-4-0 shunter was Brush Traction No. 91 of 1958. It was supplied to the Steel Company of Wales and is seen here at their Orb Works, Newport. B.E.M.

Facing page
46, 47. Front and rear three-quarter views of the same locomotive taken in June 1958, soon after delivery to the Orb Works. B.E.M.

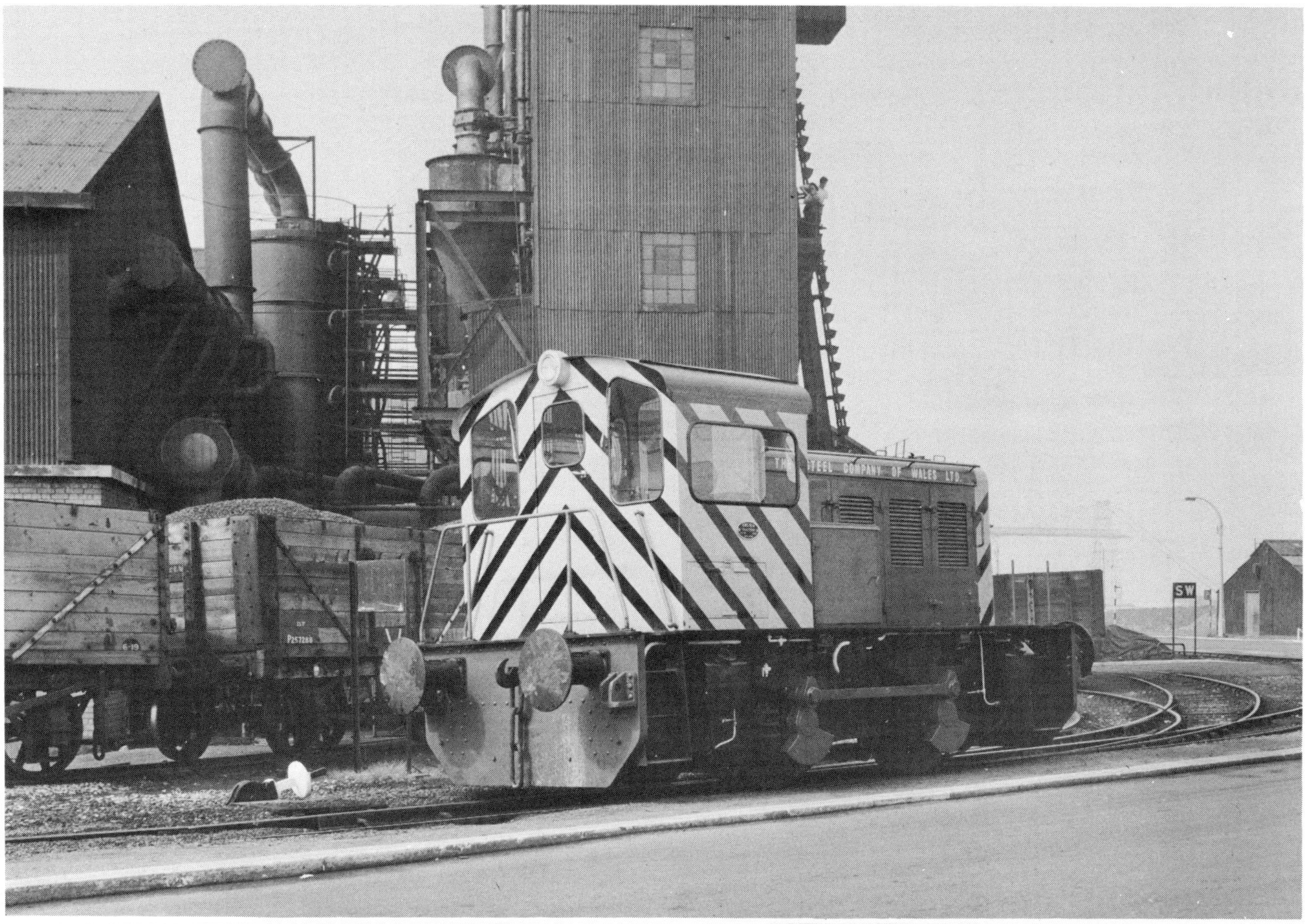
STEEL COMPANY OF WALES LTD.
SW

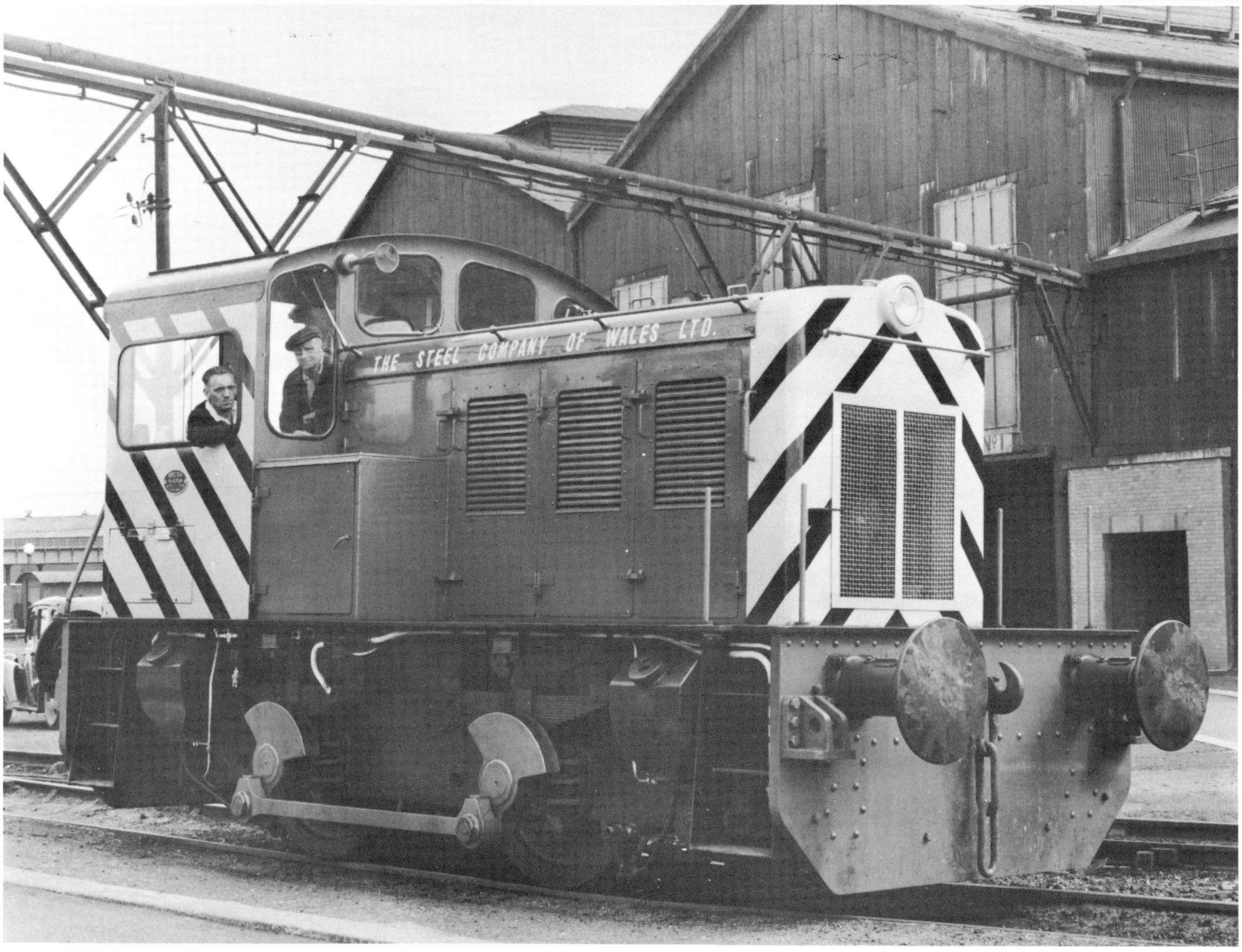
THE STEEL COMPANY OF WALES LTD.

Whilst deliveries of these locomotives took place a new order for forty Brush Type 2s was placed in July 1958. The design was basically the same, but with the engine uprated to 1365 bhp by increasing the rated speed from 850 to 900 rpm. These locomotives were classified 13/1 by Eastern Region and were Brush numbers 119–158 and B.R. D5520–59 respectively. In the meantime the intervening works numbers 99 to 118 were occupied by five 200/230 bhp Brush/Beyer-Peacock 0–4–0 shunters ordered nominally as stock items, (Beyer-Peacock 7857–61, Brush Traction 99–103, but not in numerical sequence). These units entered service in 1958/9 and can be summarised as follows:

Brush Traction	Beyer-Peacock	Delivered	bhp
99	7857	18.7.58	200
100	7861	29.12.59	200
101	7858	4.8.58	230
102	7859	18.9.58	230
103	7860	?	200

The following vehicles were also envisaged for stock construction: 104–109 400 bhp 0–6–0s, and 110–118 200 bhp 0–4–0s. The stock locomotives which were built were often out engaged on demonstration, or works shunter duties, either Brush or Beyer-Peacock. They spent some years on these duties as they themselves did not readily find customers, although orders were received for similar new units. Livery was a pale shade of orange with light green bonnet roofs. Brush monograms usually appeared on the cab sides in transfer form and also below the front radiator grille. It sometimes appeared on the cab door at the rear, in particular on number 100. One of the batch (probably 102) was named *Sprite* and received cab side monograms in plate form, in later years. These five locomotives present rather a problem of identity for although they were allotted Brush and Beyer numbers it is doubtful if ever more than one carried Brush plates and even more doubtful if any ever carried Beyer plates. The Brush plates were probably fitted for short periods only, as removal would be considered desirable when out on demonstration.

Number 99 was most likely the Loughborough-based demonstrator, which would spend its time shunting in the works when not actually on demonstration. It is also credited as being named *Sprite*, but this is very unlikely although it could have been the initial intention. In 1965 it was refurbished and sold to Skopje Steel Works in Jugoslavia, with a new 275 bhp engine.

Number 100 was used for a demonstration in a quarry near Gravesend during 1959, having its cab cut down slightly to clear an overbridge. Later it was on trial at British Railways' Mile End Goods Yard, being allocated on loan to Stratford depot in 1960. British Railways bought the locomotive in September 1960 and initially superimposed their insignia and the running number D2999 on the existing livery. Subsequently, in March 1961, it was repainted in the official green livery at Stratford Works, and classfied D2/11. Being a non-

standard locomotive its service at Stratford only lasted until April 1967 when it was withdrawn and dispatched to C. & F. Booth Ltd., Rotherham, for scrap. It may have been used there temporarily, before being cut up during October 1967.

Number 101 was one of the Brush works shunters and probably the Traction Shop's allocation for moving locomotive body shells and dead locomotives. Most of its working days were spent at Loughborough, although it may have been out on demonstration for very brief periods occasionally. It was disposed of in 1969, when it became surplus to requirements at the end of large scale locomotive construction, and was also sold to C. & F. Booth, Ltd. for scrap.

Number 102 was most probably *Sprite* from 1961 onwards, but from 1958 until 1970 was the works shunter at Loughborough, and used on general duties, which included shunting the boiler house ash wagons and various wagons brought into the works. It also assisted with Traction Shop duties and received overall black and yellow wasp stripes in 1965, when it was registered by the British Transport Commission for running on British Railways lines, to collect wagons. It carried B.T.C. registration plates, and featured as a wasp caricature, complete with wings and sting, which appeared in a cartoon on the *Brush Broadside* works notice board news sheets of the period. With the end of locomotive building and the end of rail-borne traffic in and out of the works *Sprite* was disposed of in 1970 to the Lancashire Fuel Company, in Cheshire, departing on a low loader, minus its name and B.T.C. plates, but retaining its distinctive livery. *Sprite* still survives in Cheshire and the nameplates are preserved in Loughborough, honourably retired after Brush service since 1899.

Number 103 was very likely the Manchester-based demonstrator and Beyer-Peacock works shunter. It would have been based there during the 1958–65 period; certainly it was there in 1961 and probably left on demonstration after 1/62. It was sold, with 99, to the Skopje Steel Works, Jugoslavia, before the closure of Gorton Works. It also had a new 275 bhp engine fitted and was refurbished before leaving for Skopje.

Although the correct identities of the locomotives concerned cannot be positively established, demonstrations were conducted at a number of installations, including Pilkington Glass Company, near Doncaster, in 1958, Swansea South Victoria and Prince of Wales Docks, during October 1962. One locomotive was also used in Gloucester docks during 1962 and until 7 January 1963, when a Sentinel locomotive took over for similar evaluation trials. Here the object was to find a suitable replacement for the elderly ex-M.R. 0–4–0 tanks used there. In 1961 one Brush 0–4–0 was loaned to British Railways for a trial period and numbered D9998 temporarily, latterly working at Danygraig, in South Wales, possibly until after November 1962.

Certainly these 0–4–0 shunters were very welcome at Falcon Works because the existing works shunters, which had been quite adequate up to that time were no longer so. One was a Fowler diesel-mechanical 0–4–0 named *Ace* (19425 of 1931) formerly at Petters Ltd., Yeovil; the other which inherited the nameplates from *Sprite* the 1939/40 diesel conversion locomotive, was a Ruston type 48DL four-wheel, chain-driven diesel (218049 of 1943), formerly at Mirrlees' Hazel Grove Works. Neither was a very powerful machine (70 bhp approximately) and the advent of Type 2s meant that both shunters were required in tandem for moving dead locomotives around the works, and even then a road tractor would sometimes be called upon to start the load moving for them! They were soon relegated to boiler house duties, shunting trucks of coal and ash, but by 1961 could be seen out of use on the end of the northern sidings, adjacent to the British Railways freight lines. In January 1962 they were sold for scrap to F. Berry Ltd., of Leicester.

48. One of the five 0-4-0s built by Beyer-Peacock in 1958 which were used as works shunters when not away on demonstration duties. This one, seen on the test track at Falcon Works, is believed to be either Brush Traction 99 or 101.   B.E.M.

49. *Sprite* seen near the paintshop at Falcon Works on 25 August 1956, resplendent in its new striped livery. The nameplate is one of the originals of 1899 and the locomotive the third to carry it. B.E.M.

50. Brush Traction No. 100, one of the batch of five built by Beyer-Peacock at Gorton in 1958, seen at Mile End whilst on loan for demonstration purposes during the period 1959/60. In 1960 it was bought by British Railways, which numbered it D 2999. B.E.M.

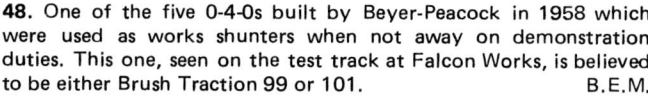

Work on the repeat order for 40 more Type 2s began late in 1958, and the first locomotive, D5520, emerged in February 1959. The outward appearance remained virtually the same as the previous examples, but very early on during the building of them the roof-mounted, four-digit route indicator panel began to replace the hinged white headcode discs mounted below window level. The changeover was applied gradually over the D5531–60 range; D5531/2/3/6/44/5 definitely had the new panels, whereas D5535/9/48/59 did not. The other difference was that, whereas D5500–19 had electro-magnetic engine speed control equipment, the newer ones were fitted with electro-pneumatic control for working in multiple. Top speed for these locomotives was 90 mph. To evaluate the future potential of the Mirrlees engine D5545 was uprated to 1600 bhp by increasing the engine speed to 950 rpm and introducing oil-cooled pistons. Delivery of the new batch took place at regular intervals up to October 1959 when the next repeat order, placed in December 1958, followed on without a production break. This order was for twenty locomotives, D5560 to D5579 (Brush 159 to 178), all rated at 1365 bhp and allocated to various depots on the Eastern Region, including Hornsey and Ipswich.

February 1959 saw one industrial order placed, for a 400 bhp shunter with 0–6–0 wheel arrangement. The National Coal Board was the customer and the locomotive was for their Eastwood Colliery at Moor Green in Nottinghamshire. A National R4AA6 engine was fitted and the locomotive was built by Hudswell Clarke Ltd., Leeds, in 1959/60, mainly due to the National Coal Board Chief Mechanical Engineer's insistence on ordering a Hudswell locomotive, as was his custom.

The design was basically Brush, as indeed was the electrical equipment. The outline followed closely some Brush-equipped Hudswell locomotives supplied to the Manchester Ship Canal Railway in 1959, which were also fitted with the National R4AA6 engine. Delivery was in 1960 and the locomotive was fitted with N.C.B. rectangular numberplates DE6, in addition to the Brush Traction 179 and Hudswell Clarke D1176 plates, already carried. It was in the colliery's service until 1975, transporting coal three miles to British Railways' Midland sidings at Langley Mill, and waste from the colliery washery to the dirt disposal site, two miles away. Unfortunately its working life came to a sudden end when the connecting rod in number two cylinder fractured, forcing the piston through the side of the

51. Many of the early Type 2s went to the Great Eastern lines of Eastern Region and D 5546 is caught here between Newport and Elsenham on the Up *Fenman*, typical of many workings on which Type 2s displaced Britannias. B.E.M.

engine. The estimated cost of spare parts and repairs was £14,000, a prohibitive figure for an already obsolete engine. Fitting a Lister engine was also considered as an alternative, but this would have cost £15,000, and the Coal Board was not prepared to spend such sums for the locomotive's repair. It was therefore condemned and sold to J. Bush Ltd., of Leabrooks, who broke it up in November 1975.

The year 1959 saw regular deliveries of Type 2 locomotives from the Falcon Works, usually two per week, and to cope with this increase extra building space was obtained by using part of the former Turbine Shop for the first time. These deliveries went to the Eastern Region; for example, at the turn of the year 1959/60 D5576/7 and the following week D5578/9 were despatched from the Works. The latter pair were of interest, ending that particular contract with two startling new liveries. Brunswick green had been the standard livery so far, but operating experience had shown that the diesels were less conspicuous to the permanent way and depot staff, because of their sombre colours and comparative quietness, compared with steam locomotives. It was decided therefore to experiment with different liveries designed to make the locomotives more conspicuous and to this end D5578 was painted a light electric blue and D5579 a vivid bronze gold. To some eyes they may have appeared excessively bright, at least to maintenance staff, as the least trace of dirt would be very apparent. It could be said, however, that with so much unimaginative colour on the railways, the change of D5578/9 was most welcome. No permanent changes resulted, but the yellow front warning patch of later years probably derived from the experiment. The next batch of Type 2s, 75 in number, ordered in April 1959, ran from D5580 to D5654 and were Brush 180–254. Deliveries again averaged two per week, from January 1960 to October 1960.

52. Back to its birthplace! Darnall's No. D 5637 standing at Loughborough Central on 4 October 1961 with the Bournemouth-York express. Although they had previously worked through with holiday relief and excursion trains this was the first occasion that a Brush locomotive worked a regular express to either Loughborough station. B.E.M.

The Turbine Shop was not the only extra space required, and extra buildings were erected between September 1959 and January 1960 on reclaimed land adjoining the meadows to the rear. These extra buildings which were used for the manufacture of locomotive superstructures, and covered 48,000 square feet, came into use during January 1960 and were officially opened on the 25th of that month. .

Another order for twenty Type 2s was received in August 1959. These were D5655 to D5679 (Brush 255–279) and were delivered between September 1960 and December 1960. Of this batch D5655–70 were uprated to 1600 bhp, as D5545 had already been, being capable of meeting Type 3 requirements in East Anglia; the remainder were the normal 1365 bhp, as before. Five months after this batch was ordered, another order for

53. D 5549 (Brush Traction 148 of 1959) on a train of mixed stock at Ipswich station. The horsebox next to the locomotive is a reminder of a once extensive traffic which has since deserted rail for road. B.E.M.

46 locomotives was placed and allocated numbers D5680–99, 5800–25 (Brush 281–326). The D5700 series was omitted as part of it was already occupied by twenty Metrovick Co-Bos. Deliveries were continuous and followed on immediately after the previous batch, from January 1961 to December 1961. So busy were the workshops that at any one time as many as twenty or more locomotives would be on site, in various stages of assembly, testing, painting, or awaiting delivery. Some of these locomotives went to Darnall and the Great Northern lines of Eastern Region and were becoming a familiar sight in ever increasing numbers.

Such was the rate of production that no industrial locomotives were being built at Loughborough through lack of space and in 1960 Beyer-Peacock were called upon again to build Brush-equipped shunters, to an order placed on 10 December 1959. This was for twelve standard 230 bhp 0–4–0 shunters for Parkgate Iron & Steel Company Ltd., of Rotherham. They were given running numbers 81–92, (Brush 327–338) and probably carried Beyer plates 7874–78/7939–45 respectively. They were ordered to replace fourteen 0–4–0 steam locomotives at the works, and then only after comparison trials and keen sales competition with other diesels. In the trials many factors were taken into account, such as operating in confined areas, shunting on tight curves and gradients, locomotive driver comfort, cab visibility, good access to and from the cab, and low engine noise level. The Brush locomotive came out on top and delivery was made during 1960/1.

In the transition period from steam to diesel some mechanical problems were encountered arising from harsh shunting, but all were overcome in due course, and the locomotives worked regularly at Parkgate until the work's gradual shutdown. They were then transferred to the Rotherham works and are now gradually being replaced by higher output diesel-hydraulics. The intention is to equip some of them for tandem operation as used elsewhere on British Railways and British Steel Corporation systems. Any single units left will have their McLaren LES6 engines removed and Rolls-Royce engines fitted instead, but the surviving units are to remain in service for some considerable time yet. Numbers 82 and 83 were scrapped in January 1972 after sustaining accident or fire damage, but not before they had been cannibalised. Numbers 81 and 87 were out of use by early 1976.

In 1961 three identical 0–4–0s were supplied to Renishaw Iron Company to an order placed on 25 April 1960. Running numbers were 21/2/3, (Brush 339–41) and Beyer-Peacock 7946–8 respectively. All were sold in 1968/9, the first two to Raine & Company Ltd., Steel Suppliers, of Newcastle-upon-Tyne, while the last one went to Italy where it probably still works, in the service of a permanent way construction company in

54. Newly completed Brush Traction No. 327 poses at Beyer-Peacock's Gorton works in 1960. It was the first of twelve 0-4-0s supplied to Parkgate Iron & Steel Company in 1960/61 and numbered 81 - 92.   B.E.M.

Rome. Another 0–4–0 was ordered for Renishaw on 8 February 1962, and was delivered later in that year. It became Renishaw 24, (Brush 443/Beyer 7873) and was sold in 1968, or 1969, to Raine & Company which operates two of the three acquired locomotives, their number 1 (Brush 339), and *Sir William* (Brush 443), the third, number 2 (Brush 340) being out of use and a source of spare parts for the others.

55. Two of the stock batch of five 0-4-0 shunters, built as Brush Traction 99 - 103 in 1958, were subsequently sold to Yugoslavia. The two (originally Brush Traction 99 and 103) were tarted up at Gorton and fitted with new and more powerful engines before being dispatched to the Skopje Steelworks, where they are thought to be still working. B.E.M.

56. In October 1962, in the Brush exchange sidings, a happy British Railways crew take delivery of D 5862, the last Type 2 to be built. B.E.M.

57. In 1959 the former Turbine Shop was adapted for locomotive building, to increase Type 2 output. In this 1961 shot *Falcon* is seen under construction on the centre road, with Type 2s on either side. B.E.M.

Meanwhile during 1961 the production rate of Type 2s at Loughborough slackened through a reduction of British Railways expenditure on modernisation, but more orders were placed despite the latter situation. The last Brush Type 2s were ordered during 1961 in two stages, D5826–35 (Brush 362–71) and D5836—62 (Brush 372–398). Deliveries spanned the period from December 1961 to October 1962 without any break in production, the last ones being delivered several weeks after the first Brush Type 4s emerged. Again these locomotives also went to the Eastern and Great Eastern lines and brought the class total to 263.

D5835 was temporarily uprated to 2000 bhp, with an intercooled Mirrlees JVS12 engine, for evaluation in regular service whilst based in the Sheffield area. It was used on a wide variety of services including Deltic diagrams from Kings Cross to Doncaster, later going to the Great Eastern lines and, although successful, it was largely overshadowed by the later re-engining programmes several years later, as indeed the 1600 bhp locomotives were. It was 1964 when British Railways ordered 50 English Electric 12-cylinder 12SV engines of 1470 bhp for installation in Brush Type 2s requiring heavy engine repairs. The Mirrlees engines had shown fatigue problems after many of the locomotives had successfully run 500,000 miles or more. This fatigue was on

the fabricated engine housing and cylinder columns and although successful modifications were effected preventing overstress, long term re-building would have been required on the class. Initially the English Electric engines were ordered to prevent large scale emergency withdrawals. Similar troubles were later experienced on the Rhodesian locomotives, but the modification held with the small number involved and Rhodesia Railways were satisfied. Ultimately the whole class of 263 British Rail locomotives was re-engined over the 1965-69 period. One advantage of using the English Electric engine was that in its application to the Brush Type 2s it was slightly under-rated, the limiting factor being the generator output and this meant that reasonably long and reliable life could be expected. Most of the original Mirrlees engines were overhauled and destined to be fitted into trawlers.

From 1966 onwards there was a gradual change to the new British Rail blue livery, just 18 months after the solitary blue locomotive (D5578) had been repainted green.

58. Another view of D 5862, the last Type 2, on the southern exchange siding on 25 October 1962. The yellow warning panel on the cab front had become standard by this time.   B.E.M.

59. In the 1972 renumbering scheme the Type 2s became Class 31, with 3 subdivisions. Those with electro-pneumatic control, like 31.235 (D 5662) seen here at Shirebrook in January 1978, were designated Class 31/1.   D. Hawkins.

In 1968 the remaining Mirrlees-engined locomotives were designated Class 30 and the re-engined ones Class 31. When re-engining was complete all became Class 31 and by the time the 1972 re-numbering scheme was implemented the Class was sub-divided as follows:

31/0 (Electro-Magnetic control)
31/1 (Electro-Pneumatic control)
31/4 (As 31/1 but with Brush electric train heat equipment)

One of the earlier 31/0s, which had been part of a batch transferred to the Western Region (to replace some withdrawn diesel-hydraulics), underwent a noticeable change. While based at Old Oak Common D5518 had, by 1969, received the roof-mounted indicator panels in place of the original discs. This came about when the locomotive was damaged in a collison and went into the works for repair to one end. A new cab was required, but an earlier pattern spare was not available so the locomotive received one of the later version ex-stock and one from D5658, which was in works too after a collision. D5518 re-emerged in patch-painted green livery, but D5658 was repainted blue and the undamaged cab from D5518 went into stock for eventual re-use. By 1977 there were 40 Class 31s allocated to the Western Region.

60. A new Type 2, D 5834, waits for the British Railways crew to come and collect it on 1 March 1962.   B.E.M.

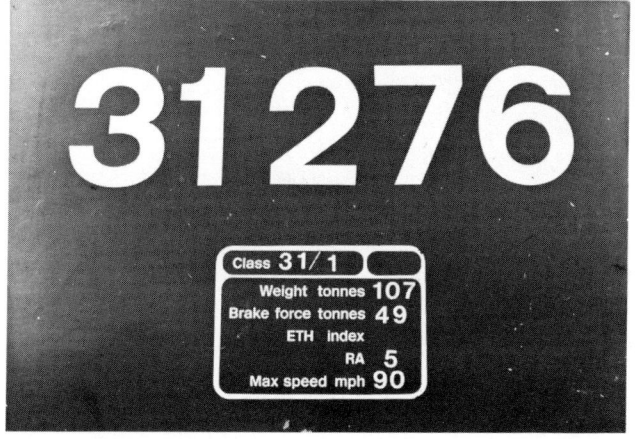

61. A typical Brush Traction worksplate, as fitted to D 5595.
D. Hawkins.

62. The current style of transfers, as seen on Class 31/1 locomotive 31.276 (D 5806).   D. Hawkins.

The class stayed intact until October 1975 when 31.150 (D5568) was withdrawn from service following

an accident and period of store at Doncaster. The accident took place at Corby Tunnel, near Gretton in Northamptonshire, in September 1975 when a brake van and 38 coke wagons ran loose out of control from near the British Steel Corporation sidings at Corby. With no possible means of either diverting or stopping them, they gathered momentum and entered the tunnel, two miles on, at speed. Unfortunately, 31.150 was approaching the tunnel from the opposite direction and was struck head on by the runaway wagons just as they came out of the tunnel. The cab of the locomotive was crushed and the driver killed. When 31.150 was recovered from beneath the pile of wagons, the damage was found to be so extensive as to prevent economic repair. It was allocated at the time of the accident to March depot.

In July 1976 the first report of an intended class 31 withdrawal came when 31.018 (D5500) was stored at Stratford pending removal for preservation in the National Railway Museum at York. 31.018 arrived at York Museum on 8 January 1977 and was on exhibition until early March, when it left for Doncaster Works for restoration to its original green livery. Eight more class 31s were reported stored, week ending 9 May 1976, these being 31.001/7/9/10/1/2/4/6 and by September 31.001/9/10/1/6 and 31.018 were officially withdrawn from stock, followed soon afterwards by 31.007/12/4. Of these last three 31.007/12 were cannibalised as a source of spare parts for the remaining class 31/0s.

During April 1977 the withdrawn 31.014 was announced as one of four class 31 locomotives converted to mobile electric train heat generators for use on Eastern Region. The prospect of further conversions was expected if they proved successful.

63. A head-on view of 31.235 (D 5662) gives a very clear picture of the front end detail of the Type 2. This photograph was taken at Shirebrook depot on 22 January 1978.　　　D. Hawkins.

64. No. 31.203 (D 5627) backs down onto its train at King's Cross, during the period when electrification work was nearing completion.　D. Hawkins.

65. A long rake of "Presflo" cement wagons enters Eastfield Yard, Peterborough, on 20 May 1977, hauled by 31.151 (D 5569). J.A. Howie.

66. Another Type 2 in action. A train of car transporters passes through Doncaster station on 29 April 1977, behind 31.232 (D 5659). D. Hawkins.

FALCON

In April 1959 Brush Traction 280 was allotted to an entirely new venture, the Company's *Falcon* project. A very careful study had been made of the feasibility of producing a 2800 bhp lightweight Type 4 locomotive. As Brush had already been supplying electrical equipment for 2500 bhp 1-Co-Co-1 locomotives being built by British Railways at Derby, the project was the next logical step to meet British Railways' possible future requirements. The Railway was contemplating expanding its diesel fleet with higher output units, but with a much lighter axle load of 19 tons. Two other companies were also preparing prototypes in anticipation of orders; these were the English-Electric 'DP2', and the Birmingham Railway Carriage & Wagon-Associated Electrical Industries Companies' *Lion*.

It was decided that *Falcon* would have two engines, each rated at 1440 bhp at a speed of 1500 rpm, because at this time no single 2800 bhp engine was available and it was an opportunity to demonstrate the advantages of high-speed engines made by Bristol-Siddeley, based on Maybach design. Since 1956 Brush had had exclusive United Kingdom manufacturing rights for Maybach engines, and Bristol-Siddeley was an associated company within the Hawker Siddeley Group. The Group had absorbed Brush in 1957, so since the project was a private venture it was desirable to have as much equipment as possible manufactured by companies within the Group. One advantage gained with using two engines and associated main generators was that in the event of a failure of one set the other set of equipment could operate independently. The design was prepared in consultation with British Railways in order that the locomotive would be a prototype for general requirements and it would be possible to test run it on British Railways lines without any major alterations.

67. *Falcon* under construction, early in 1961. The nature of the bodywork, with its load-bearing side members, is clearly evident. Note also the transporter bogies on which the shell is temporarily mounted.   B.E.M.

Facing page
68. One of *Falcon*'s two Bristol-Siddeley Maybach 1440 h.p. engines being lowered into position at a late stage in construction.   B.E.M.

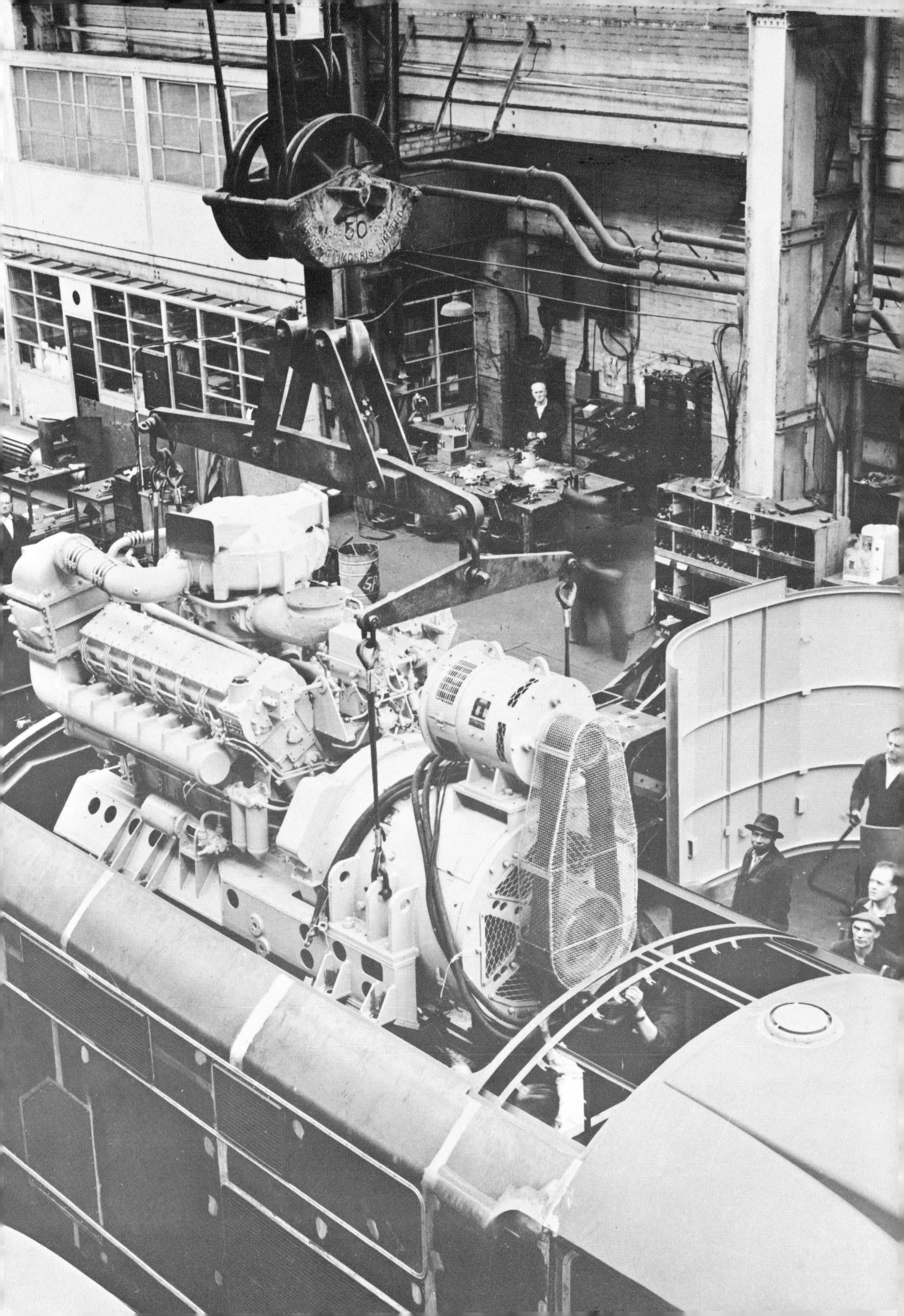

Late in 1960 construction commenced and proceeded until September 1961, when it was completed. Externally *Falcon* was a magnificent sight, being painted in a two-tone light green scheme and bearing a painted Falcon motif midway along each side. Running number D0280 was painted on the cab sides in contemporary British Railways style. A balanced and tasteful effect was achieved with the grouping of louvres in the bodysides, despite the fact that these were plentiful due to the duplication of power units. The time had not yet arrived when louvres could be placed in the roof sections, because the Railway still required some measure of side access to engine compartments. Nevertheless, to lighten the locomotive it had been decided that the floor should not carry all the load, so the sides were built as an open lattice frame to assist in weight carrying, thus forming an integral framework with the floor, though the sheeting applied to the body sides was not stressed. The Railway made possible this solution by not stipulating sideways removal of the power unit as they had in previous specifications, so heavy weight-bearing underframes were avoided. The cab design was a smoother version of the Brush Type 2 outline and one which was developed, imitated and continued as standard even to the present Class 56. *Falcon* was an immediate favourite with Brush personnel and much pride was generated by its later exploits. Its main details were as follows:

Wheel Arrangement	Co-Co
Maximum Tractive Effort	60,000 lb
1 hour Tractive Effort	31,500 lb
Continuous Tractive Effort	28,500 lb
Maximum Speed	100 mph
Weight in Full Working Order	115 tons
Overall length	68ft 10in
Overall width	8ft 9in
Overall height	12ft 9in
Fuel capacity	1,400 gallons
Minimum Curve Negotiable	4 chains
Axle Load	19¼ tons

69. Gleaming in new paint *Falcon* stands outside the Turbine Shop on 18 September 1961, ready to make its first appearance on the main-line.   B.E.M.

ENGINE DATA

Bristol-Siddeley Maybach (two) MD 655
Vee-type 12-cylinders
1440 bhp at 1500 rpm continuous rating, with pressure charging and intercooling
Bore 7.28in.
Stroke 7.88in.
Compression ratio 15.5:1

MAIN GENERATORS (TWO)

Six-pole compensated type with three windings separately excited and self excited shunts and a differential series winding.
Self-ventilated and mounted on extension arms from engine bedplate.
Continuous Ratings: 910 kW, 493v, 1845 amps.
915 kW, 610v, 1500 amps.

TRACTION MOTORS (SIX)

Four pole, force ventilated, axle-hung, nose-suspended type.
Continuous Rating: 373 hp, 493v, 615 amps at 704 rpm.
One hour Rating: 365 hp, 455v, 660 amps at 630 rpm.
Bogies: Commonwealth cast steel frame type.

70. A close-up of *Falcon* as it prepares to leave on a trial run. The same general front-end design was also used on the Brush Type 4, for which *Falcon* was sometimes mistaken when she later became part of British Railways stock. B.E.M.

71. *Falcon* seen on the test track at Loughborough in March 1962. The Great Central main-line is visible in the background. B.E.M.

72. The original transfers soon gave way to handsome polished aluminium emblems cast in high relief, and similar nameplates. This photograph of them was taken on 3 April 1962. B.E.M.

After *Falcon* emerged from Loughborough it underwent trials on British Railways London Midland and Eastern Regions, transferring to the Great Eastern lines during the early part of November 1961, and returning to the works several times for routine checks. Early in the new year *Falcon* was moved to the Western Region and on 6 February 1962 it featured in an assault on the famous Lickey Incline, where banking had been the order of the day for many decades. Indeed the Midland Railway had built a special 0–10–0 steam engine in 1919 wholly for this purpose. The incline of 1 in 37.7 was first attempted by a steam engine which stalled, amid clouds of smoke and steam; then came *Falcon*'s turn. With eighteen coaches and the Western Region's new Hawksworth dynamometer car recording details, a total of 628 trailing tons, it successfully accelerated from a dead stand on the incline and continued until it was well clear of the summit. A tank engine trailed hopefully at the rear, but was disappointed. This was repeated three times daily and tests were also conducted with *Falcon* hauling mineral trains well in excess of 500 tons gross, the current maximum allowed on the incline. *Falcon* had achieved 100 mph on the level with 273 tons trailing, and 75 mph with eighteen coaches (600 tons) during running tests.

73. In February 1962 trials were carried out on the Lickey Incline, with the Western Region dynamometer car and an eighteen coach train. *Falcon* was able to restart this mammoth load from a dead stand on the notorious bank and clear the top without difficulty.

B.E.M.

The following week *Falcon* was working in the South-West, again with the Western Region dynamometer car, on the Swindon to Plymouth run. West of Newton Abbott it tackled inclines of 1 in 36 and 1 in 47 with loads of 500 tons. On 13 February Dainton Bank was surmounted with 571 tons trailing. By April *Falcon* had been back to Loughborough for inspection and emerged with one visual change; a new relief cast aluminium Falcon motif now appeared on the body sides, a more imaginative embellishment than the previous painted motif.

Falcon next went to the Eastern Region and was allocated to Sheffield Darnall depot, from where it operated the *Sheffield Pullman*, travelling 3,200 miles per week gaining running experience for the Region's service requirements.

In the Autumn of 1962 *Falcon* was transferred to freight duties, in particular coal traffic working two double trips between Langwith Junction and March, or New England yards. By the beginning of 1963 the total mileage logged by *Falcon* had reached 120,000, all accumulated over an eighteen month period. After continued use on Eastern Region in 1963, *Falcon* returned to Brush and lay out of action until late 1964, its tests completed. It had been rumoured that *Falcon* was to be re-engined with different types of engines for evaluation, but in the event the Maybach engines were retained; being identical to those being fitted to *Hawk*, subsequent interchange would be possible should the need arise. Late 1964 saw *Falcon* undergo complete renovation, to emerge at the end of January 1965 with a new coat of British Railways Brunswick green.

Trials were now over and *Falcon* had helped pave the way for large Type 4 orders for Brush, eventually totalling 512 units, from both Loughborough and Crewe Works. Not yet life-expired, *Falcon* was destined to work on Western Region for the rest of its existence. The loan of the locomotive was under a joint agreement, dated 1 January 1965, whereby the Railway would run it and carry out light repairs, while Brush would undertake any major electrical repairs, or maintenance. *Falcon* was allocated to Bristol Bath Road for crew training and went into revenue earning service on Paddington-Bristol diagrams. In 1968 the new British Railways diesel classification system designated *Falcon* as Class 53. In 1970 British Railways approached Brush with a view to buying *Falcon* at scrap value, to which the Company agreed on condition that after a specified period they would sell the locomotive for scrap. In December 1970 *Falcon* was taken into British Railways stock, repainted rail blue, with overall yellow ends, renumbered 1200 and converted to air brake only. On re-entering service during February 1971 it again went to Bristol Bath Road, being transferred to Cardiff Canton Depot in October 1972 for working Newport Docks to Llanwern duties.

Type 2, D 5540, in original green livery, passing Rotherwood Sidings on a passenger working. J.C. Lane.

The 8.15 Paddington-Barnstaple, hauled by Type 2 No. 31.412, passing Tiverton Junction on 6 July 1974. J.C. Lane.

The driver of 31.243 picks up the single line staff at Maltby Colliery South signal box on 12 October 1974. J.C. Lane.

The 12.35 Paignton-Birmingham approaching Whiteball summit on 26 July 1975, behind Type 2s 31.304 and 31.265.
J.C. Lane.

A Type 2 in green livery, D 5523 runs light out of Liverpool Street Station, August 1969.   J.A. Senior.

A loaded coal train, with 31.149 at the head, lumbers onto the main line at Whitwell (Derbyshire) on 6 October 1976.
J.C. Lane.

74. After a lengthy trial period on various lines and duties, *Falcon* returned to Loughborough for renovation and repainting in British Railways standard green livery. It was then hired to British Railways Western Region which used it for some ten years before withdrawal, in 1975, for breaking up. This photograph was taken on 27 January 1965.   B.E.M.

In 1973 it was still on freight duties, but based at Ebbw Junction, Newport. During Autumn 1974 it arrived mysteriously at Loughborough, settling on a siding at the rear of Loughborough Midland Station. *Falcon*'s arrival caused quite a lot of local speculation and consternation as to its intended future. Apparently it had arrived, months after a national power crisis, with British Railways hoping to resell it to Brush as a standby generating plant! Certainly it could not enter the works without difficulty as the rail links had been severed, but after several days the Railway realised its error and *Falcon* returned to its former duties.

Almost a year later, in August 1975, *Falcon* went into store, being officially withdrawn from capital stock on 5 October and sold to Cashmore Ltd., Newport, for scrap. The locomotive arrived at the scrap-yard for breaking up on 26 March 1976, despite preservation appeals and cutting up was completed within days of arrival. *Falcon*'s mileage totalled 635,000 of which 515,000 had been accumulated on the Western Region.

THE TYPE 4 ERA

While *Falcon* was under construction an important engine development had taken place in which the Sulzer 12LDA 28 12-cylinder engine had been successfully uprated to 2750 bhp and designated 12LDA 28A. The forerunners of this engine had been fitted to the Peak class 1-Co-Co-1s in the form of the 12LDA 28A (2300 bhp) and 12LDA 28B (2500 bhp). The Peaks however were heavy, their 138 tons requiring extra non-powered weight-carrying axles and long bogies, not a desirable feature, particularly when negotiating marshalling yard humps. These disadvantages had caused British Railways to reconsider the design and postulate a single power unit, and a light-weight body, mounted upon shorter 3-axle bogies. To this end, therefore, in 1960 British Railways sought a suitable design and builder for their requirements, which were largely embodied in *Lion* (D0260), the new Sulzer-engined prototype being developed by Birmingham Railway Carriage & Wagon – Associated Electrical Industries, and about to undergo main line trials. This design did not meet the Railways' requirements fully, but was considered to be a promising one, and the makers were asked to co-operate in building part of a fleet of over 500 units. For reasons which have not been made public nothing came of this invitation, so the Railway approached Brush for suitable design studies in which some of *Lion*'s better features were to be incorporated.

Brush responded with several draft versions, offering different power plants and a willingness to install whatever electrical equipment the Railway required. Negoti-

ations proceeded in conjunction with the Chief Mechanical & Electrical Engineer's Department, which eventually chose the Sulzer engine, and equipment previously fitted to the Peaks. Part of the reason for this choice also lay in the fact that some of the equipment had already been ordered for more Peak locomotives. This equipment was to be housed within a new lightweight, monocoque, stressed shin, box-type body, with triangular framework at each end to transfer end shocks to the bodysides. The same negotiations with British Railways involved a licensing agreement enabling the Railway to build many of the locomotives at Crewe Works, concurrently with Loughborough, using Brush-designed and manufactured electrical equipment. Agreement was reached by the parties, resulting in a pilot order being placed on 28 February 1961 for twenty Type 4 locomotives to the new design, in lieu of ten Peaks on order from the Railways' own workshops, which were cancelled. This reduced the final total of Peaks to 193.

The twenty new locomotives were allotted running numbers D1500–19, (Brush 342–61) originally intended partly for the Peak series. Construction proceeded swiftly and, with the new type of body construction, traditional methods of body-building virtually ceased, so a certain amount of re-education into the new methods took place at Loughborough. The first unit took shape in the workshops during the earlier half of 1962 and emerged complete in September, just as the last few Type 2s were nearing completion. Externally D1500 had very clean lines, with a cab design similar to that fitted to *Falcon*. All louvres were mounted in the roof section, to retain the qualities of the new body design, and light-weight materials were used in the cab roof, notably aluminium and glass fibre. The new design was 5ft shorter than *Falcon*, through the use of one power unit. The livery was British Railways two-tone green, a familiar sight up to the mid-1970s, when the now ubiquitous blue gradually replaced it. In retrospect the choice of fitting Sulzer engines was regrettable, indeed British Railways acknowledged this

75. The body shell of D 1500, the first Type 4 (Brush Traction 342), begins to take shape. It is seen mounted on transporter bogies for transfer between shops. The former Great Central main-line appears in the background.　B.E.M.

finally in 1967, but at the time it was considered by them to be desirable. One extra and useful provision on the first twenty locomotives was that the train heating generator was mounted on a common shaft with the main generator. This had been part of the Type 4 general specification, but was subsequently deemed non-standard by British Railways on further construction, which was perhaps another regrettable decision in view of the intermittent unreliability of steam heating equipment, and later conversions to electrical train heating. Main details of the Type 4:

Wheel Arrangement	Co-Co
Maximum Tractive Effort	55,000 lb
1 hour Tractive Effort	33,000 lb
Continuous Tractive Effort	30,000 lb
Maximum Speed	90 mph
Overall Length	63ft 6in
Overall Width	8ft 9¾in
Overall Height	12ft 9⅜in
Minimum Curve Negotiable	4 chains
Weight in Working Order	114 tons
Maximum Axle Load	19 tons
Fuel Capacity	850 gallons
Wheel Diameter	3ft 9in
Bogie Wheelbase	14ft 6in
Distance between Bogie Pivots	37ft 0in

76. The body shell of D 1500 undergoing strain tests to measure the distortion under load. The photograph was taken in 1962 in the former Turbine Shop. B.E.M.

77. Another view in the Turbine Shop as the 2750 h.p. Sulzer engine is lowered into the body of D 1500 in April 1962. Some of the final year's production of Type 2s can also be seen. B.E.M.

Main generator:

Eight pole compensated 3-field type, with separate and self-excited fields and a series decompounding winding. (The latter used also for engine starting).

1798 kW 844v 2130 amps
1805 kW 970v 1860 amps   1150 rpm

Traction Motors: (Six)

Continuous Rating: 368hp 422v 710amps, at 766rpm

1 hour Rating: 362 hp 391v 762 amps, at 698 rpm

Each 4-pole force-ventilated axle-hung type.

Train heat generator affixed to main generator

8-pole shunt type 800v 320 kW Continuous rating at 690 to 1150 rpm.

Although not light-weight, manganese cast steel 'Commonwealth' bogies were fitted to avoid excess weight and air brake equipment was also fitted.

78. On 3 September 1962 the first Type 4 moves on to the departure siding, prior to handing over to British Railways. Notice that the running number is carried on a small white panel attached to the cabside, but within a few days it had been removed and the number painted on the side in the usual style. B.E.M.

79. By 19 September D 1500 had received the standard British Railways livery and numbering and is seen under the loading gauge, close to the Up platform of Loughborough station. B.E.M.

80. D 5858 and D 1500 pose together on the approach lines to the test track, 20 September 1962. This was a fairly rare occurrence as Type 2 production was ending at the time Type 4 started to appear. B.E.M.

81. D 1500 went to Western Region during February 1963 for dynamometer trials. It is seen here on Dainton Bank with the new Hawksworth dynamometer car, which was designed and built specifically for testing diesel locomotives in service.   B.E.M.

Facing page
82. During the big freeze of January 1963 British Railways crews prepare to take over D 1506 and D 1507 at the exchange sidings outside Falcon Works.   B.E.M.

The first twenty, D1500–19, were delivered between September 1962 and March 1963, to the Eastern Region, where they operated on the main East Coast route. After completion, early in September 1962, D1500 underwent trials, with up to fifteen coaches, between Syston and Cheadle Heath, on the London Midland Region, then in mid-September went to Cricklewood to be inspected by British Transport Commission officials. After the handing over ceremony D1500 went to Finsbury Park depot on the Eastern Region, where it was initially allocated for service. On 10–11 October the locomotive underwent comparison trials with the Deltics between Kings Cross and Doncaster, hauling trains of up to 385 tons, and in November it was loaned to Western Region for trials, being allocated to Swindon depot. These trials with the Western Region Hawksworth dynamometer car and a seventeen coach test train, took place during February 1963, between Swindon and Plymouth. Two test stops and restarts were undertaken on Dainton Bank in each direction. Also in

February D1500 was tested on the famous Lickey Incline with nineteen coaches and a dynamometer car, totalling 690 tons. Two stops and restarts were successfully made and the resident Bromsgrove steam banker, 9F 2–10–0 92079, had a disappointing day, trailing hopefully some distance behind the train. Routine testing and pre-delivery trials of the Brush Type 4s usually took place on the Midland line north and south of Loughborough, with a visit to Derby Works for commissioning and weighing. The test run was from Derby (Chaddesden) to Cheadle Heath and back, southwards through Spondon and Loughborough to Syston, from where the train returned to Derby.

D1501 was delivered late in October 1962 and joined D1500 at Finsbury Park depot, until being transferred to New England in 1963, on crew training operations in preparation for freight working. The initial deliveries were rather slow because minor problems encountered in service with D1500–2 caused modifications to be carried out at Loughborough during the building of the others. In the first few months the locomotives were used on a variety of duties, for example D1503 was employed on crew training between Doncaster and Leeds during January 1963, D1505 underwent dynamometer trials on the Scunthorpe line later the same month, and D1502 was also on crew training duties, hauling parcel trains, between Newcastle and Carlisle, whilst based temporarily at Gateshead depot. In March D1510 went to Haymarket depot in the Scottish region for crew training, whilst D1513 was also on the Scunthorpe line undergoing dynamometer runs. When D1516 emerged it underwent roadrailer tests on the Great Northern main line and D1517 operated the *Sheffield Pullman*. By April there were ten Brush Type 4s available for Class 7 freight working northwards out of Kings Cross.

On 1 January 1962 a second Type 4 order was placed with Brush for 30 locomotives, to be numbered D1520–49 (Brush 413–442). D1520 was completed in June 1963 and deliveries to the Eastern Region continued until October 1963, with an average of six locomotives emerging each month. This batch differed from the first batch, with the omission of electric train heating equipment, mainly resulting from a British Railways decision to commit themselves for the immediate future to continue using steam heating. The

chance was lost, therefore, of having a large standard class all equipped similarly, the later conversions, when electric train heating was adopted meant that some main engine output had to be diverted from traction use to heat trains. In place of the electric train heating, therefore, a Spanner Mark 3B oil-fired steam heating boiler was fitted, not altogether a wise move. Other changes were concerned with modifying the vacuum brake equipment, in the light of operational experience with D1500–19.

The next batch of Brush-built Type 4s was ordered on 4 September 1962 and numbered D1682-1706 (Brush 444–468). Modifications were again made, mainly to the axle design, in order to aid maintenance and better running performance. Deliveries were to the Eastern and Western Regions, from October 1963 until January 1964, but in the case of D1702–6, these were delayed by the experimental fitting of French-built Sulzer 12-cylinder, 2650 bhp 12 LVA24 Vee-type engines running at 1050 rpm. This fitting was for evaluation tests in regular service of the new type of engine developed in France. One of these locomotives was exhibited at the Royal Festival Hall in London during April 1965. Unfortunately with the passing of time the Vee-engine proved inferior to the twin bank type, but they did survive long enough for the locomotives to be classified Type 48 in 1968. D1682/3 were the first members of the class to be allocated to the Western Region,

83. D 1730, seen on 10 April 1964, was one of the first Type 4s to be spray painted. Note the Western Region route restriction code below the works plate, and the Western Region pattern lamp brackets. B.E.M.

initially being employed on crew training while based at Old Oak Common depot. The allocation generally for the Western Region was to be employed on the Paddington to West Midlands express services, but D1690/1 were sent to Cardiff (Canton) depot, being the first allocation to South Wales. By January 1964 more Type 4s began to emerge, this time from the Railways' workshops at Crewe, and from this time onwards the class began to expand rapidly. These locomotives were destined for London Midland Region and were all Brush equipped.

The next batch, D1707–81 (Brush 469–543) were ordered on 28 September 1962, and delivery followed on from D1701 without a break, extending into October 1964. Delivery was at regular intervals, but due to delivery outstripping paintshop capacity some locomotives went to Derby for final painting. Some modifications were again incorporated. First of all, from D1714 onwards, the traction motor electrical interconnection was changed from the previous series-parallel arrangement to all parallel. This was carried out to reduce the voltage on the main generator (and so reduce the likelihood of commutator flashover) and also to improve the electrical conditions which followed any wheelslip. This naturally meant a new main generator design, along with new associated control gear to cope with the increased current, so the main generator rating became 422v 4260 amps instead of the previous 844v 2130 amps, the rotational speed being unchanged at 1150 rpm. From D1758 onwards Mark 1 automatic air brake equipment for the train was installed, in addition to the vacuum only type previously fitted. This installation

84. A British Railways crew climbs aboard D 1731 to take delivery on 14 May 1964. B.E.M.

85. A Brush Type 4, No. D 1738, near Royal Oak with a Down express in 1964. Note the Western Region type lamp brackets. B.E.M.

was made in response to a British Railways decision in 1963 to introduce Freightliner trains for fast and reliable freight traffic and, although the scheme was much delayed, the modifications required on the locomotives were worked out and incorporated on the production line as quickly as possible.

On this batch two notable visual changes occurred. First, from D1730 onwards, spray painting was introduced to facilitate increased production because brush painting was proving too long a process. The resultant finish, although somewhat more dull or flat than before, when new, proved extremely durable in service. The other change was with D1733, when it was selected in May 1964 to take part in an experiment which was to have a lasting impact on the general railway scene, both in the visual and the passenger comfort sense. The experiment was called the XP 64 train. This experiment was basically intended to evaluate passenger comfort, but there was a desire to project British Railways as a corporate identity, and to this end a new livery of light blue was applied in this one instance, along with the then unusual but now familiar double arrow symbol, in place of the heraldic lion and wheel. The train made a number of demonstration runs but sometimes the effect was spoilt when D1733 was not available to haul it, resulting in a green engine and blue train.

The next batch D1782–1841 (Brush 544–603) was ordered on 22 July 1963 and delivery commenced, again without a break from the previous batch, in November 1964 and continued until April 1965, some being delivered out of sequence. Indeed 1965 was the year when production reached an all time record of 112 locomotives for the whole twelve months, with a few still being painted at Derby and thus deviating from the delivery sequence. From the very first locomotive of this batch a Universal Boiler compartment was introduced to accommodate any of the three types of steam heat boilers currently being used; this was dependent upon which one was standard in the Region to which the locomotive was allocated. Previous units had had Spanner boilers for Eastern Region service. From D1807 onwards, modification to the automatic air braking system was carried out, to improve the accessibility, which had proved troublesome; this modification resulted in the equipment being designated Mark 2.

Other additions had already appeared by now and two in particular stand out. Firstly, there was the provision of additional automatic warning system equipment for locomotives destined for the Western Region and, secondly, there was the automatic slow speed device, which enabled Merry-go-Round trains to pass through power station sidings at controlled low speed, allowing for wagon weighing and load discharging through hopper doors. This allowed smooth and frequent block trains through, without resort to yards and shunting operations. The electric unit which controlled the slow speed gave accurate speed measurement not possible with previous mechanical or electrical devices.

The last order for Type 4s was placed on 24 March 1964, and was for a hundred locomotives, which were numbered D1862–D1961 (Brush 624–709 and 610–623 respectively). Delivery commenced in May 1965, without any production gap from the previous batch. This brought the Brush-built total to 310 units, to which could be added the British Railways Crewe-built 202, making a grand total of 512 Brush, or Brush designed and equipped, diesel-electric locomotives of one general outline, the largest group of general purpose locomotives in Europe. The running numbers allotted to the Crewe-built examples were D1550–1681, D1842–1861, D1962–1999, D1100–1111. Delivery from Loughborough slowed down considerably during 1966, as the following figures show: D1862 to D1925, May to December 1965; D1926 to D1950, January to August 1966; D1951 to D1959, August 1966 to February 1967.

86. In the spring of 1964 British Railways launched its XP64 experimental train. D 1733 was chosen for repainting in the new blue livery which was the prototype for the now ubiquitous BR Rail Blue. The locomotive is seen at the head of the XP64 train passing through Loughborough at high speed on 20 May 1964.
Facing page   B.E.M.
87. No less than ten Type 4s in varying stages of construction in the former Turbine Shop at Falcon Works. The right-hand locomotive on the farthest row is one of the Rhodesia Railways Co-Cos. B.E.M.

Type 4, D 1842 with a train of loaded hopper wagons passes under the West Coast main line at Arpley Junction, Warrington, on 23 March 1973.

J.C. Lane.

Type 4 No. 47.142 entering Morton in Marsh station with the 16.15 Worcester-Paddington express on 7 July 1974.　　　　J.C. Lane.

The 13.40 Aberdeen-Glasgow express, hauled by 47.038, pulls away from Gleneagles station on 28 May 1977.　　　　J.C. Lane.

Type 4 No. 47.149 descending Harbury Bank at the head of a Freightliner, on 27 May 1975. J.C. Lane.

Type 4 No. 47.095 emerges from Whiteball Tunnel with the 12.26 Paddington-Paignton express on 26 July 1975. J.C. Lane.

A loaded Merry-go-Round train, with Class 56 No. 56.002 at the head, passes Foxlow Junction signal box, Staveley, on 22 June 1977. J.C. Lane.

88. D1573, one of the Crewe-built Type 4s, is seen immediately after arrival at King's Cross with a train from Leeds. Note the 55A (Leeds Holbeck) shedplate, a poignant reminder of steam days.

At this time Brush had started other traction work and some attention was diverted from the last Type 4s and also, as often happens after long production runs, material shortages occurred, all combining to produce a prolonged tail-off. D1938 differed from its companions by being fitted with push-pull equipment for Paddington to Birmingham services, an arrangement which avoided end of journey running around by locomotives.

By the time this locomotive had gone into service the Railway had decided to work the route with diesel multiple-units instead, so D1938 never made practical use of the equipment. At some point during August/September 1966 the changeover to applying the then new rail blue livery occurred, D1953 probably being the first example to receive it, along with British Railways/Sulzer Type 4s and a British Railways/Sulzer Type 2, the former then in the Falcon Works being refurbished. Such work had been undertaken at Loughborough for a while during 1965/6, as the Railways' workshops were fully occupied with other work. The new livery was officially recorded for posterity by D1958, when it was photographed in the oft-used location of the southern exchange sidings. It was D1958, much modified on paper, which featured in the advance publicity for 56.001 during 1975!

The very last pair of Loughborough-built locomotives (D1960–1) was completed in mid-1967, but delivery to London Midland Region's Western lines was delayed until July 1967 and May 1968 respectively. This was because these units had been selected for experiments with a new type of electric train heating. A brushless a.c. generator was secured to the free end of the main generator on a common shaft, and without extensive alteration to it. It had two power outputs, one of 110 volts and the other 800 volts, both of which were rectified to d.c. The former supplied the auxiliary equipment, to a capacity of 55 kW, and the latter 320 kW for train heating. The control and rectifier equipment was fitted neatly between the a.c. generator and the engine compartment bulkhead, and was cooled by the generator air intake flow. It was possible to fit this new equipment without engine removal and without disposing of the steam heating equipment then still necessary on British Railways.

89. Another Crewe-built Type 4 (D 1586) seen in undercoat in September 1964, while at the head of an Up test train passing through the Lune Gorge, just south of Tebay.　　　　B.E.M.

90. The lengthy Type 4 construction run was almost over when the Rail Blue livery was introduced. Consequently, not many new locomotives were turned out in blue from Loughborough. D 1958 provided the first opportunity to photograph it at the works on **14 January 1967.**　　　　B.E.M.

91. Compare this head-on view of a Class 47 (formerly Type 4) with that of a Class 31 (Type 2) on page 42. Here 47.169 (D 1764) is seen at Shirebrook depot on 22 January 1978.   D. Hawkins.

92. A group of Class 47s (47.445, ex-D 1561; 47.530, ex-D 1930; 47.138. ex-D 1730; and another unidentified) standing at King's Cross on 1 June 1978.   D. Hawkins.

This was another practical application of a.c. generation, as opposed to d.c., a trend in which Brush played such an important part. It had probably been the Railways' intention to allocate D1960–1 to Western Region, as the red route indication transfers had been affixed, but considerable running was noted in the Derby, Nottingham and Leicester areas. D1961 was used on the Midland lines to Cricklewood during 1971, in conjunction with Derby Research Department tests of the experimental electric train heating and coach air conditioning. This was the period prior to the general introduction of Mark IId coaching stock, fitted with Brush motor-alternator sets. Also during this time further Brush Type 4s were converted to electric train heating, as featured in D1960–1.

In 1968, after the final demise of steam, the locomotives were designated Class 47 generally and Class 48 for the D1702–6 members, with the Sulzer 2650 bhp engines, although by 1972 the latter had all become Class 47 on re-engining. The development of these latter engines was the enlarged version, fitted to *Kestrel* in 1967. The class designation introduced at the end of steam did not have any significant effect until the general renumbering of most classes on British Railways, which was introduced during 1973, although the dropping of the D prefix between those years did produce hybrid styles and liveries particularly on well worn numerals. When the renumbering did come it used the following sub-groups according to equipment fitted:

47/0 Locomotives fitted with steam heating boiler.

47/3 Locomotives without any train heating equipment.

47/4 Locomotives fitted with dual, or electric, train heating.

The 47/4 variety had increased in numbers after some service time had elapsed, as too had the equipping of more locomotives with train air brakes, and the Western Region based ones with British Railways standard Automatic Warning System.

Early in 1965 Western Region began to experience difficulties with the Sulzer engine after some time in service. These problems had not been foreseen, due to the comparatively limited amount of prototype work which the uprated engine had done in service, and the locomotive as a whole had been ordered straight from the drawing board without several years prototype or initial batch experience. Under these conditions, therefore, it had not been foreseen that stresses caused by vibration would in turn cause the engine mounting brackets, which were made up of fabricated plates on the generator end, to fracture. The source of the vibrations was in the crankcase webs, which had been lightened after the uprating of the 12LDA 28B engine, to bring the engine weight within the required Type 4 specification. This followed complaints from British Railways that their weight limit was being exceeded, so the formerly thickened webs were lightened by Sulzers. To deal with the problem it was decided to thicken the offending webs once more, and replace the engine

mounting brackets with a new weldless design and with the stresses effectively distributed. British Rail also stipulated that further new Sulzer engines must have ten year guarantees against structural failure. Temporary derating of the locomotive had been considered, but some of the more exacting requirements encountered in regular operation precluded this, as services could not be maintained. A year later lesser fractures appeared in the crankcase and also the camshaft guide housings. These troubles probably caused British Railways to steer away from Sulzer engines in the long term and

93. A close-up of the current styles of transfer used for running number, shed code and other salient details. The photograph was taken at Shirebrook depot on 22 January 1978.   D. Hawkins.

94. A typical Brush Sulzer worksplate, as fitted to D 1786 (47.305).   D. Hawkins.

95. First came petrol-electric, then diesel-electric, and what is this? Steam-electric? No, it is actually 47.197 (D 1847) at York on 29 April 1978, working an excursion formed of Southern Region steam-heated stock, for which the locomotive's boiler is keeping a good head of steam.   D. Hawkins.

during 1966 the hoped for further Type 4 order for Brush did not come. The Sulzer engine troubles led to an initial British Railways ban on further new purchases and the outcome was the English-Electric Class 50 (D400–449), introduced from late 1967 onwards. These locomotives were the direct descendants of the DP 2 prototype which had been *Falcon*'s competitor a few years previously.

The Sulzer Vee-engines fitted to D1702–6 paved the way for the *Kestrel* engine, but although they were used on intensive freight diagrams and three of them had each accumulated over 8000 operating hours and 100,000 miles in two years, no real advantage was realised. The engines were removed between December 1969 and June 1971, the locomotives then conforming generally to the Class 47 standard. Individual dates were as follows:

D1702 12/69	D1703 11/70	D1704 6/71
D1705 4/71	D1706 11/70	

96. A scene at Godley Junction on 30 March 1978, as 47.338 (D 1819) sets off with a train of bogie bolsters it has just taken over from a Class 76 electric locomotive.   D. Hawkins.

It is sad to relate that two Brush-built Type 4s, as well as two Crewe-built examples, were written off by the Railway due to severe accident damage. Although it had been proved beyond doubt that the structural design was extremely rigid and capable of withstanding considerable impact shock, there were obviously conditions in which the locomotive could be damaged beyond repair. The first Brush-built Type 4 to go was D1734 of Bristol Bath Road depot. It was barely eight months old, when on 11 January 1965 it was working the 03.56 Saltney to Pontypool Road loaded freight train, consisting of 46 wagons and a brake van, weighing 775 tons. The driver of D1734 failed to stop at a stop board, which was situated at the top of the 1 in 100 downhill gradient approaching Coton Hill South yard, near Shrewsbury, and the train ran away out of control. It ran into the Up goods loop at speed, overran the loop exit signals and went through the trap points at 20 mph, despite a late brake application. The locomotive was derailed and continued for 72 yards beyond the trap points, demolishing Coton Hill South signal box, and sustaining much damage to its No. 1 cab in the process. D1734 was so badly damaged that economic repair could not be effected and it was cut up at Crewe Works by April 1965.

On 8 April 1969 Brush-built D1908, allocated to Cardiff Canton depot, also succumbed, when it had been in service for four years. It was involved in the Monmore Green accident near Wolverhampton. A four-car electric multiple unit, the 14.15 from Wolverhampton to Coventry, ran through signals set at danger and crossed from the Up to the Down line at about 45 mph. It collided head-on with D1908, which was standing with the 06.30 special freight from Chesterfield to Wolverhampton, consisting of thirty-two loaded steel wagons. The leading coach rode up through the No. 1 cab of D1908 and into the auxiliary compartment behind, where it ruptured one of the fuel tanks and also fouled the 25 kV overhead catenary. Fire broke out, which further damaged the locomotive before the local fire service could arrive. D1908 was officially withdrawn in August 1969 and cut up at Crewe Works by the following October.

The first of the Crewe-built examples to go was D1671, then named *Thor*, on the night of 16/17 December 1965, when hauling an empty stock train. Heavy rain had caused a landslip near Bridgend into which D1671 ran, the locomotive then fell over on to the other track. Almost immediately a double-headed freight train crashed into it, causing severe damage. Afterwards it was towed away to Bridgend sidings and subsequently scrapped by Hayes & Co. The official withdrawal date from British Railways stock was November 1966.

The other Crewe locomotive to be destroyed was D1562. This unfortunate event occurred on 13 March 1971 at Haughley, near Stowmarket, when it was hauling the 9.30 Liverpool St.-Norwich. A brake application caused sparks to ignite accumulated oil and dirt on one of the locomotive's bogies. The resultant fire in turn overheated one of the fuel tanks which exploded, spraying the engine compartment with burning diesel fuel. The fire damage was so great that the locomotive was declared a write-off; the official withdrawal date was June 1971 and the remains were cut up at Crewe Works.

97. On 4 April 1978, a loaded Merry-go-Round train, hauled by 47.305 (D 1786) passes the former Shirebrook station, which closed in October 1964. D. Hawkins.

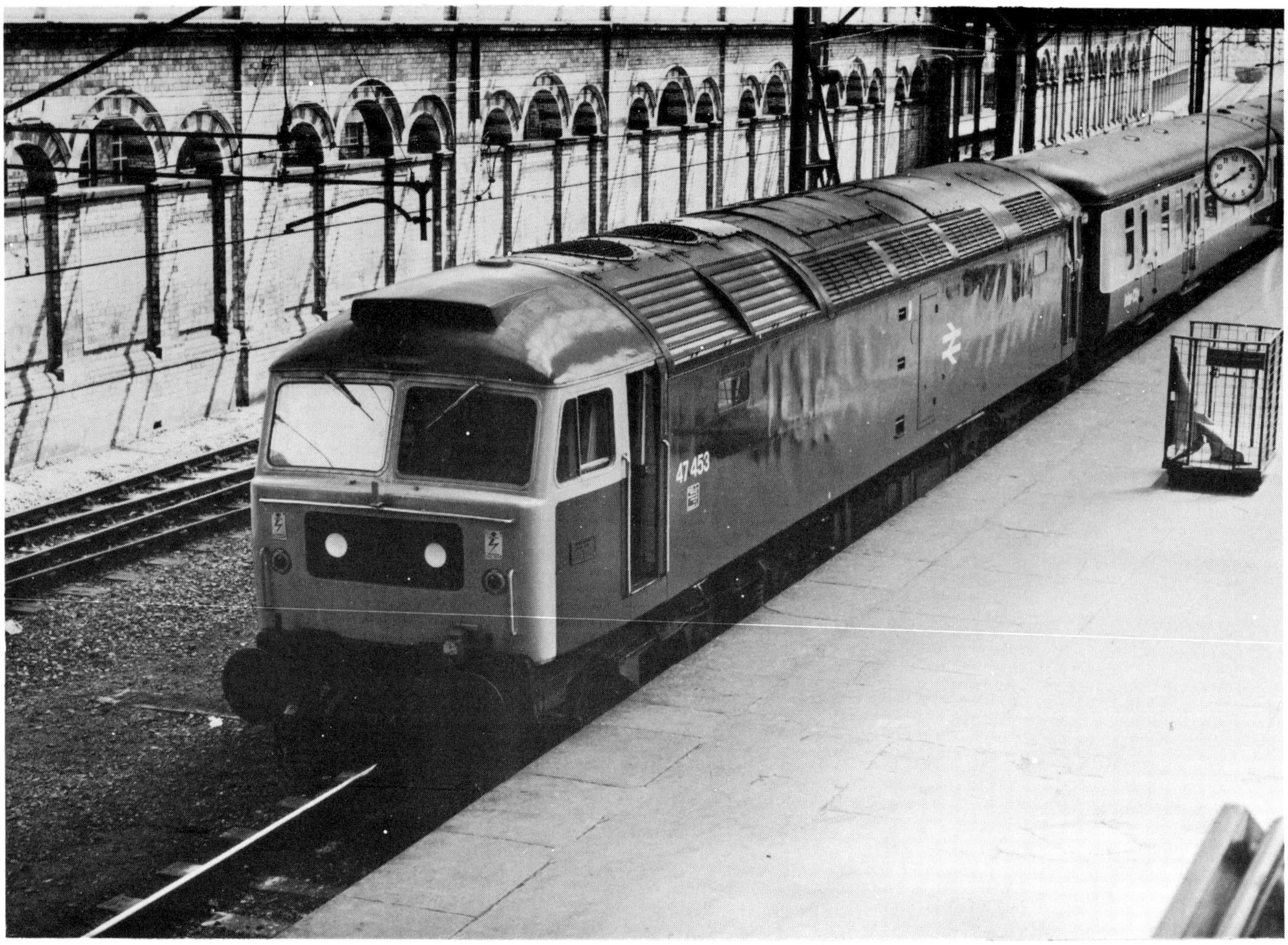
47 453

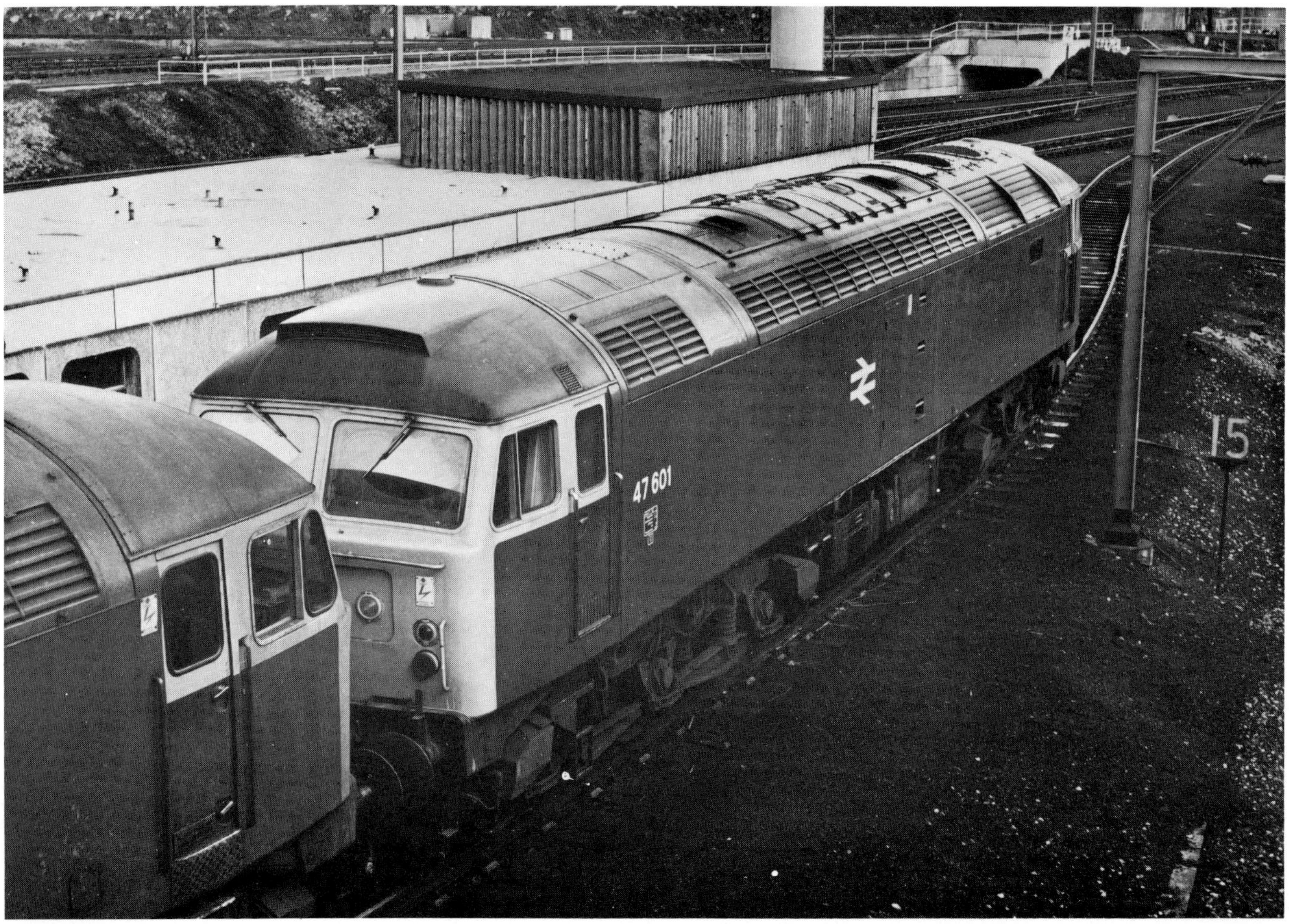
47 601
15

On 23 May 1970, the fire which damaged the Britannia tubular bridge across the Menai Straits isolated three Class 47s at Holyhead, D1724, D1940 (ex-Brush) and D1851 (ex-Crewe). As a result these locomotives had the unusual distinction of being transported by sea between two home destinations, Holyhead and Barrow-in-Furness, so that they could continue in revenue-earning service on the mainland.

One unusual but very practical event took place in January 1976 when Stratford based 47.155 (D1748) was separated from its bogies and transported by road on a low loader to West Thurrock Power Station, in Essex. It was installed there as a temporary excitation source for a turbo-alternator after the failure of the usual auxiliary generator. It was hired, at very short notice and delivered power to the equivalent of a sustained 60 mph in running service.

Facing page
98. A sunny day at Crewe on 19 June 1977 sees 47.453 (D 1571) waiting to leave at the head of a Down Inter-City express.
D. Hawkins.

Facing page
99. In 1976 one of the Crewe-built Type 4s, 47.046 (formerly D 1628) was re-equipped with a General Electric 3250 h.p. motor and higher capacity electrical equipment. Renumbered 47.601 it was based at Tinsley depot, where the photographer caught it on 22 January 1978. It remains the only example of its type.
D. Hawkins.

100. One of the two Type 4s specially decorated with Union Jack, silver roof and white wheel rims for working *The Jubilee*. The ill-fated 47.163 (D 1757) waiting to depart Norwich Thorpe in the late afternoon of 25 October 1977.
J.A. Howie.

During 1977 British Rail Eastern Region decided to celebrate Jubilee Week, 8–11 June, by temporarily naming the 8.30 Liverpool Street-Norwich and 15.48 return working *The Jubilee*. For this duty two Loughborough-built locomotives, 47.163/4 (ex-D1757/8), were specially prepared, each having a silver painted roof, buffers and couplings, and white wheel rims. On each bodyside was painted a large Union Jack and a special train headboard was fitted, depicting two Union Flags and the Queen's portrait.

During the early 1970s British Railways had considered refurbishing the Class 47 locomotives with 3250 bhp General Electric 16RK3CT diesel engines and higher output Brush electrical equipment. One Crewe-built example (47.046, formerly D1628) was selected for conversion in 1973, and during 1974 equipment was on order for installation. In March 1975, however, a change of policy directed the project into a prototype for the Class 56 freight locomotive and the original plan was dropped.

The conversion took place at Crewe Works and after much delay the locomotive emerged as 47.601 early in 1976. It went to Derby and was released for crew training purposes in May 1976. Trials were conducted with the locomotive based at Tinsley Depot, Sheffield. 47.601 remains unique and may well provide a basis for Class 47 development, but only time will tell since there has been no indication of future policy resulting from this project.

THE 'HAWK' AND 'KESTREL' PROJECTS

In 1964 Brush Traction No. 710 was allotted to a unique and farsighted locomotive experiment, the *Hawk* project. Although not a new locomotive it was used for prototype work for the second time in its life.

It was originally conceived by the London, Midland & Scottish Railway in 1946 as a diesel capable of light and short haul duties and was at first fitted with a Davey Paxman 827 bhp engine and British Thompson Houston electrical equipment. It was finally completed in 1950 by the North British Locomotive Company of Glasgow, as their works number 24613 and British Railways number 10800. It ran trials in Scotland and was then sent to London Midland Region for evaluation before being transferred to Southern Region in 1952. By 1955 it was on the Eastern Region and shortly afterwards returned to the London Midland, being based at Rugby shed until withdrawn in August 1959. It was set aside and languished, awaiting disposal, until 1962, when it was selected as an ideal mobile test bed for

101. *Hawk* seen in Falcon Works on 6 November 1962 while it was being converted. The new Bristol-Siddeley-Maybach engine has already been fitted. B.E.M.

Brush research into commutatorless traction motors and main generators.

During that year, after British Railways agreed to release it, it was taken into the Falcon Works and refitted with a Bristol-Siddeley-Maybach MD655 diesel engine of 1400 bhp, developed at 1500 rpm. Directly coupled to the engine was a Brush 950 kW, 8-pole, 3-phase brushless a.c. generator, with a maximum voltage between lines of 1325 volts. Frequency was proportional to speed with a maximum of 100 Hz. The a.c. generator output was rectified by a Westinghouse silicon diode bridge rectifier to provide a variable voltage d.c. This d.c. supply was inverted into variable frequency a.c. by thyristor control and then fed into four 3-phase a.c. squirrel cage induction motors, which were the old traction motor shells, re-adapted specially for this purpose. The variable frequency was controlled by the driver and this in turn altered the positive to negative switching rate of the thyristors.

Facing page
102. Number 10800 *(Hawk)* undergoing static tests on 3 June 1963, while standing on the Research Department siding. B.E.M.

Facing page
103. After the static trials new fittings were installed on 10800 during 1964. B.E.M.

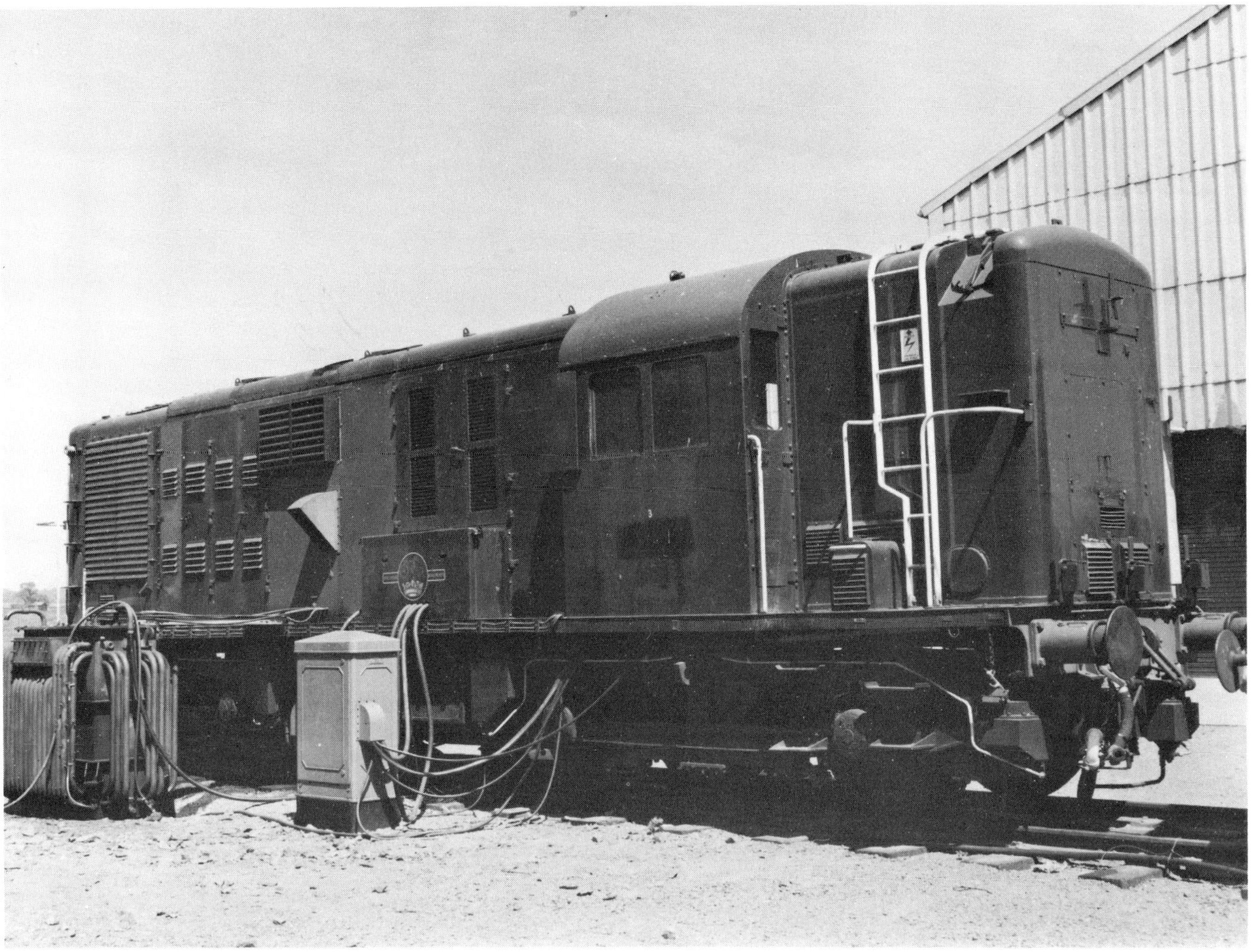

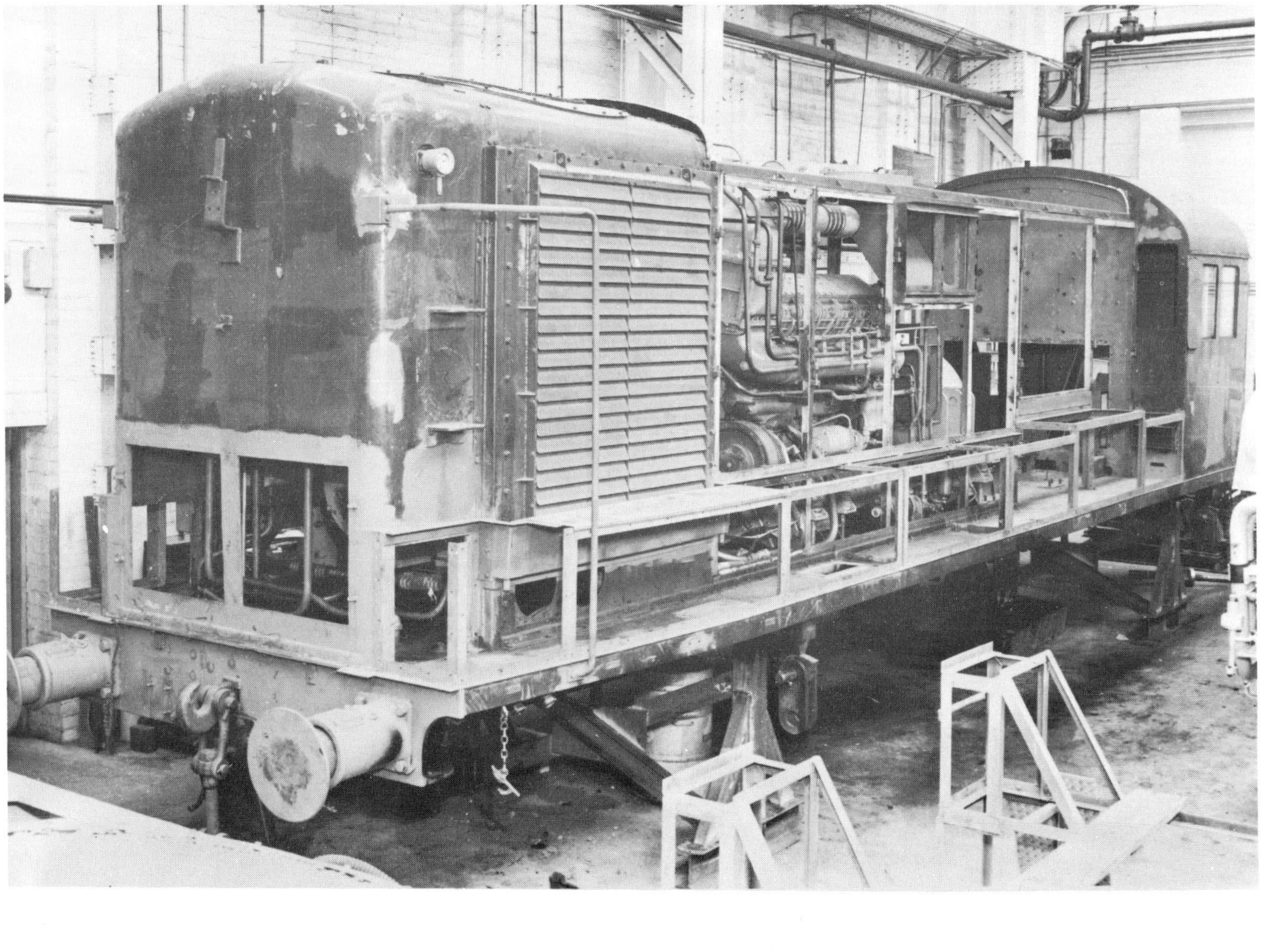

During 1963 10800 was parked on the Brush Research Department's siding, and connected electrically to a cubicle which linked the locomotive with monitoring equipment within the Research Department building for the preliminary static testing and research. In 1964, after completion of these tests, 10800 underwent the final stages of conversion, such as superstructure modifications, overhaul and repaint. The locomotive emerged during the latter part of 1964 in British Railways light green livery with 10800 on the cabsides and the legend 'Research Locomotive' below. The lion and wheel emblem also appeared, as British Railways participated financially in the experiment, although the locomotive was now Brush-owned. It was officially designated by the name *Hawk* but never bore it; indeed the only legend which appeared was 'Research Locomotive' already mentioned.

Early in 1965 *Hawk* went to Rugby for commissioning tests and trials. It also spent some time on the former Great Central line between Nottingham and Leicester, being stabled at the latter shed. Runs along this line were generally confined to the 10.00a.m. to 2.00p.m. period, when *Hawk* could be given track occupation for test trips. Visits were often made to Falcon Works for modifications and some electronic rebuilding. At East Leake provision had been made to use the Plaster Board exchange sidings, but this was never actually

required. At that time the official maximum speed was 30 mph, as successful running had been achieved using one traction motor only, but unofficially a speed of 56 mph had been reached.

The project had moderate success but difficulties were experienced with the invertors. It is thought that induced currents and harmonics in the circuitry caused invertor instability and in turn frequency control instability. The project had petered out by 1968 due to the need for more capital investment to continue the research and it is believed that an American concern had volunteered to take it over. The offer was tactfully declined, so *Hawk* was left in the works, next to the test house, and rotted away steadily, isolated on its own section of track, surrounded by healthy weeds and numerous rejected objects. The miners' strike and accompanying power shortage of 1972 prompted the removal of the engine and radiator section to be used as the prime mover of an emergency works electricity supply. The rest, except the bogies, was cut up on the spot soon afterwards and sold. The engine, radiator and bogies remained at the Works, but in May 1976 the bogies were cut up for scrap and the traction motors stored. In July 1976 the radiator was moved to the Research Department for use elsewhere.

104. A rear view of 10800 shortly after leaving the Paint Shop, late in 1964. Although officially known as *Hawk* the name never appeared on the locomotive, though the legend Research Locomotive was painted on the cab side sheets.   B.E.M.

The project was useful in some respects, particularly by applying to *Kestrel* some of the techniques which had been mastered. In the long term it was the use of an a.c. generator which altered the method of electric power generation in main line diesel locomotives, from the conventional d.c. Indeed, in 1977 a.c. generators, i.e. alternators, are regarded as standard equipment.

During the period when the Type 4s were being produced, thoughts turned to the next logical step in diesel-electric locomotive development, a locomotive of higher power output. By 1964 not only Brush but also British Railways Western Region and Sulzer were interested in a locomotive in excess of 3,300 bhp. Brush wanted to develop the Type 4 concept further, while British Railways were anxious to increase operating speeds and also avoid uneconomic double-heading of expresses; the latter was also to be avoided on heavy freight trains. Sulzer were setting their sights on further development of their LVA 24 engines with a 16-cylinder version, of 3946 bhp. British Railways had produced a draft specification to meet their own requirements for a high powered locomotive, suitable for heavy freight and express passenger duties, which should not exceed 126 tons in working order, and both Sulzer and Brush endeavoured to meet this requirement, the project being initiated in July 1965.

A single engine was called for as weight restrictions precluded the use of two, and the only one then available was the Sulzer 16LVA 24, which was untried. To meet the higher power output, this Vee-engine had been designed to run at a higher engine speed and mean effective pressure, and give a comparatively low weight for that power. Also it did not restrict the space available within the locomotive unduly. A prototype engine had been under test at Sulzer's Winterthur Works, and had been submitted for an International Union of Railways 840 hours endurance test in 1966. Late in 1966 a

second identical engine was produced for installation in a British prototype locomotive. This locomotive was *Kestrel*, a private venture of Brush, which was embarked upon in early 1965, partly to provide test facilities for the Sulzer Vee-engine and the newly-developed Brush a.c. main generator; the latter was under development in an effort to avoid the use of heavier d.c. generators.

105. In 1968 the experimental work with *Hawk* was abandoned and the locomotive dumped near the Test House. Left to the elements the paintwork faded and peeled and in 1972, after the salvable parts had been removed, the remains were cut up for scrap on the spot.

G. Toms.

106. Below we see it at Falcon Works in its prime, together with D 1806 (dispatched on 5 December 1964) and *Falcon*. *Hawk* and the refurbished *Falcon* both made their debut in January 1965.

B.E.M.

Kestrel was given the running number HS 4000, (Brush 711) denoting both its main sponsor, Hawker Siddeley, and its metric horsepower rating. The new locomotive was scheduled for completion in early 1967 and by February/March 1966 two of the traction motors had been tested at their full rating. Two a.c. main generators were also under construction, one for *Kestrel* and one to be supplied to Winterthur to complete the tests on the first engine. The general design was based on the Brush Type 4 and only differed from it externally in the semi-streamlined, rounded cabs at each end, adding three feet to overall length of the Type 4. *Kestrel*'s main details were as follows:

Maxiumum Speed	125 mph
Continuous Speed	110 mph
Length over Buffers	66ft 6in
Total Wheelbase	51ft 8½in
Maximum Height	13ft 0½in
Maximum Body Width	8ft 9¾in
Wheel Diameter	3ft 7in
Minimum Radius Curve	264ft
Fully Laden Weight	126 tons (estimated)
Maximum Axle Load	21 tons
Diesel Fuel Capacity	1000 gallons

Main Generator:

10 pole, 3-phase a.c. Salient pole alternator, with integral a.c. brushless exciter. Continuous rating 2520 kW at 410v, 1100 rpm, 91.6 Hz.

D.C. Traction Motors (six):

Series wound, parallel connected, axle mounted, nose suspended, force ventilated. Continuous rating 515 hp, 504v, 830 amps, 681 rpm.

Dynastarter:

D.C. generator driven, via gearbox, from diesel engine to provide auxiliary power when running, although main function was to start diesel engine electrically from batteries. Continuous rating 47.6 kW, 110 volts at 1125 rpm.

Auxiliary Trainheat Alternator:

8 pole, 3-phase, with integral brushless a.c. exciter. Driven from the dynastarter through a flexible coupling. Electronic voltage stabilizing fitted. Continuous rating 534 kVA, 680 volts a.c. at 2750 rpm.

Brakes:

Independent air braking on locomotive only. Vacuum or air for train braking. Dynamic braking integrated with mechnical braking under single control.

The main generator was a 3-phase a.c. alternator and this extended the use of a.c. output as demonstrated in *Hawk*. This output was rectified integrally within the alternator with the use of silicon diode rectifiers, and the ensuing d.c. supply was fed into the traction motors as in previous practice. Nevertheless, electronic control equipment was used extensively and a lot of *Hawk*'s experimental work was put to further use. Additionally, auxiliary electrical equipment was made up of a.c. induction motors instead of the normal d.c. motors. Weight reductions on all the a.c. machines helped keep the overall weight to a minimum.

107. Flanked by two of the later Type 4s, *Kestrel* takes shape in the Turbine Shop. This shot was taken on 23 January 1967.　　B.E.M.

Construction proper started in 1966, and by November 1967 *Kestrel* was complete, although a little overdue because the braking resistors were resited from beneath to within the body, thus avoiding the exhausting of hot air at platform level and exhausting it at roof level instead. When *Kestrel* did make its appearance it was a magnificent sight, and most attractively styled too; a far cry from the Ceylon locomotives of the early 1950s. There was a very pleasing golden yellow scheme for the upper bodywork and an equally attractive and practical chocolate brown for the lower areas. The two colours were separated by a thin white line, passing all the way round the locomotive at waist level. The then new Hawker Siddeley symbol and HS 4000 appeared on the cabsides, and the legend *Kestrel* on each bodyside, in white letters on the yellow portion, a truly magnificent looking locomotive.

After the preliminary checking period *Kestrel* went to Derby on 22 January 1968 for weighing and produced an overweight result of 133 tons 6cwt. It was sent to London shortly afterwards and on 29 January was at Marylebone Station for the official handing over and unveiling ceremony. When this had duly taken place, with its attendant publicity run, *Kestrel* was scheduled to work on freight turns. The decision to operate on these duties first was because the 126 tons overall weight target had been exceeded, and it contravened the coincidental British Railways reconsideration of preferring a 20 tons axle load on 100 mph schedules involving nose-suspended traction motors. The freight duties were to be undertaken on Eastern Region between Shirebrook and Whitemoor, hauling coal trains and although a regular Type 4 load of 1500 tons gross was hauled, the full capacity of *Kestrel* could not be utilised because of the difficulty of marshalling heavier trains regularly.

Early in May 1968, following brief returns to Loughborough for modifications and routine checks, *Kestrel* worked on hopper train runs between Stoke-on-Trent and Crewe. It was also loaded with twenty coaches, totalling approximately 670 tons, and hauled them on test runs between Crewe and Carlisle, a minimum speed of 46 mph being recorded over the notorious Shap Summit. Afterwards dynamometer trials were undertaken in the Derby area.

On 13 May *Kestrel* was transferred to the Mansfield-Whitemoor duties on a regular basis, the diagrams being as follows:

7J31	11.09	Mansfield Colliery Sidings-Whitemoor (arr. 14.20)
7P31	15.10	Whitemoor-Mansfield Colliery Sidings (arr. 18.23)
7J07	19.40	Mansfield Colliery Sidings-Whitemoor (arr. 22.53)
5P07	23.45	Whitemoor Down Yard-Thoresby Colliery Junction

108. Gleaming in new paint, the 4000 h.p. *Kestrel* stands completed inside the works in November 1967.　　　　B.E.M.

109. This close-up of the cab section, taken in January 1968, gives a clear idea of the smooth curves evolved by the design consultants for the front end. A new rectangular style of works plate (BT711 of 1967) was also used for the first time.   B.E.M.

110. *Kestrel* on its first demonstration run from Marylebone, January 1968.   B.E.M.

Typical workings were two round trips every week-day, covering 360 miles and clocking up 15 engine hours on them. The average load was 1500 tons full, and 750 tons empty on the return journey, using about 75 per cent of the available power, at a maximum of 35 mph. Up to 30 June 1968 8,290 miles had been covered on these duties. During July and early August *Kestrel* was still working freight on Eastern Region and this period concluded with a 2028 tons test run, which took place between Mansfield and Lincoln. The aim was to determine whether one locomotive could handle such a load, instead of the usual two. On the outward journey a successful start was made under wet conditions on the 1 in 150 Boughton Bank, with automatic wheelslip control functioning correctly. An even better start was made during the return working on the 1 in 120 Marham Bank.

During mid-August *Kestrel* went to Derby and was based there for dynamometer trials which were under-taken with the former London, Midland & Scottish Railway Mobile Test Unit providing electrical load. These trials lasted from 12 to 27 September, after which *Kestrel* returned once more to Loughborough for minor adjustments, inspection and further static testing. In October it undertook speed trials on a circuit between Derby, Crewe, Nuneaton, Leicester and Derby, and after these returned to the Shirebrook-Whitemoor run in late November. By the end of the year *Kestrel* had accumulated 1731 engine hours and 26,000 miles in revenue-earning service.

While *Kestrel* was on those duties Brush was prepar-ing new bogies, basically identical to those fitted to the Brush Type 4s, but modified to accept a hydraulic handbrake system, to replace the original heavier bogie type, with overhung equalising beams. The lighter bogie brought *Kestrel*'s axleload to 21 tons; just over, but nearer to British Railways 100 mph axleload limit for passenger work on Eastern Region. *Kestrel* returned to Loughborough during February 1969 to have the new bogies fitted and emerged after static tests during late March.

111. *Kestrel* seen at the head of a twenty-coach test train between Crewe and Carlisle, in May 1968. This and other trials enabled a number of minor snags to be identified and put right.   B.E.M.

Before taking up express passenger duties *Kestrel* was employed on crew training duties for some weeks, followed by a brief visit to Stratford works. The locomotive was finally in service during October 1969 on inter-city services on the East Coast Route between Kings Cross and Newcastle. It headed the 16.45 out of Newcastle, before undertaking a regular passenger diagram, the 07.55 from Kings Cross and 15.45 return from Newcastle.

After two months of passenger duties *Kestrel* returned to Shirebrook during January 1970 for examination, but with the intention of returning to the East Coast Route later in February. A change of policy by Brush diverted the locomotive from passenger work because the Railways' Civil Engineer had imposed a 75 mph restriction on its operation on the East Coast Route. This meant *Kestrel* was unable to work to its full capacity in the passenger role, so it was sent to Hull for working the Hull-Stratford freightliner diagrams. A regular run was the 19.35 from Hull, returning with the 02.30 from Stratford. During weekdays *Kestrel* was stabled at Dairycoates depot, but each weekend had to visit Tinsley depot for maintenance, as the former was not a main line diesel depot.

112. To allow it to work passenger trains *Kestrel* was fitted with new bogies which brought its axle load down to 21 tons. *Kestrel* is here seen at Falcon Works in February 1969 being lowered onto the new bogies. B.E.M.

On 1 June 1970 *Kestrel* entered Sulzer's works at Barrow-in-Furness for engine examination, overhaul and modification, remaining there until 3 September, when it went to Tinsley depot for modification and attention to the electrical equipment by Brush engineers. The latter completed, *Kestrel* went to Shirebrook once more on 21 September for freight duties, and was based there throughout the winter months, until mid-April 1971. During these last months the news broke that *Kestrel* had been sold to Russia.

The seeds of this sale probably originated back in March 1969, when a Soviet delegation of locomotive engineers had visited Falcon Works and seen *Kestrel* while it was there for its bogie change. This visit must have generated Soviet interest in the locomotive for during 1970 Brush was invited to exhibit *Kestrel* at the Moscow Rolling Stock Exhibition, held from 1 to 20 July 1971. After the Hither Green accident in November 1967, British Railways had gradually moved away from the idea of a single-engined 4000 hp unit, likewise the overseas prospects for such a locomotive had also waned, so Brush was reluctant to incur the considerable expense of shipping *Kestrel* to Moscow. The idea of selling *Kestrel* was put to the Russians, and to this they agreed.

113. *Kestrel* entered passenger train service during October 1969 and this shot shows it about to leave King's Cross on 20 October, with its first regular scheduled passenger service. Unfortunately, two months later, following a change of British Railways policy, the locomotive had to be returned to freight working.   B.E.M.

The previously-mentioned accident at Hither Green involved a fractured rail near a joint, and it led British Railways engineers to rethink the whole subject of axle loads and maximum speeds. The one long term outcome which really sealed *Kestrel*'s fate in Britain was the Railways' revised policy of splitting the two basic functions of freight and passenger duties, thus destroying *Kestrel*'s dual purpose role. Policy then dictated a course which led to the High Speed Train and the heavy freight locomotive of Class 56. Thus, despite the fact that *Kestrel* did all it was required to do and more, British Railways' rethink killed any possibility of home orders, and after totalling 136,646 miles *Kestrel* was sent to Crewe Works on 22 April 1971 for overhaul, fitting of bogies regauged for Soviet use, and additional Soviet requirements.

On 11 June 1971 *Kestrel* was loaded on board a Russian ship at Cardiff Docks, and exhibited at Moscow soon afterwards. Subsequently it operated on the closed-loop test track of the All-Union Rail Transport

Scientific Research Institute, at Shcherbinka Station, 30km from Moscow, and also ran between Leningrad and Tanmir, being fitted with a prominent headlight on one cab roof for the purpose. Since then no concrete information has emerged as to the fate of *Kestrel* itself, although there are signs that descendants are about to emerge within Eastern Europe.

Indeed, in East Germany Class 132 had already used the *Kestrel* internal works principle and it was even fitted inside a bodyshell derived from British Railways' Class 47, after Russian examination of the Clayton Type 4s, supplied to Cuba in 1965/6. From this adaptation of *Kestrel*'s internal equipment, the East German Class 118 had its bodyshell selected to house the *Kestrel* equipment instead. The resultant marriage will be designated Class 119.

Facing page
115. Minus the bogies, which were loaded separately, a floating crane hoists *Kestrel* aboard the M.V. *Krasnokamsk,* on 11 June 1971. B.E.M.

116. After featuring at the Moscow Rolling Stock Exhibition in July 1971, *Kestrel* went to the Soviet Railways Research Institute at Shcherbinka, near Moscow, where this photograph of it on the test track was taken, probably in 1972. The fitting of a large roof-mounted headlight at only one end of the locomotive suggests that it had not been used in normal service, nor has any report of it in action been received since this photograph first appeared. B.E.M.

114. With no future for it in Britain, Brush decided to sell *Kestrel* and offered it to the Soviet Union. The offer was accepted and the locomotive was shipped to Leningrad. Here it waits on the dockside at Cardiff before being loaded onto the Russian M.V. *Krasnokamsk.* B.E.M.

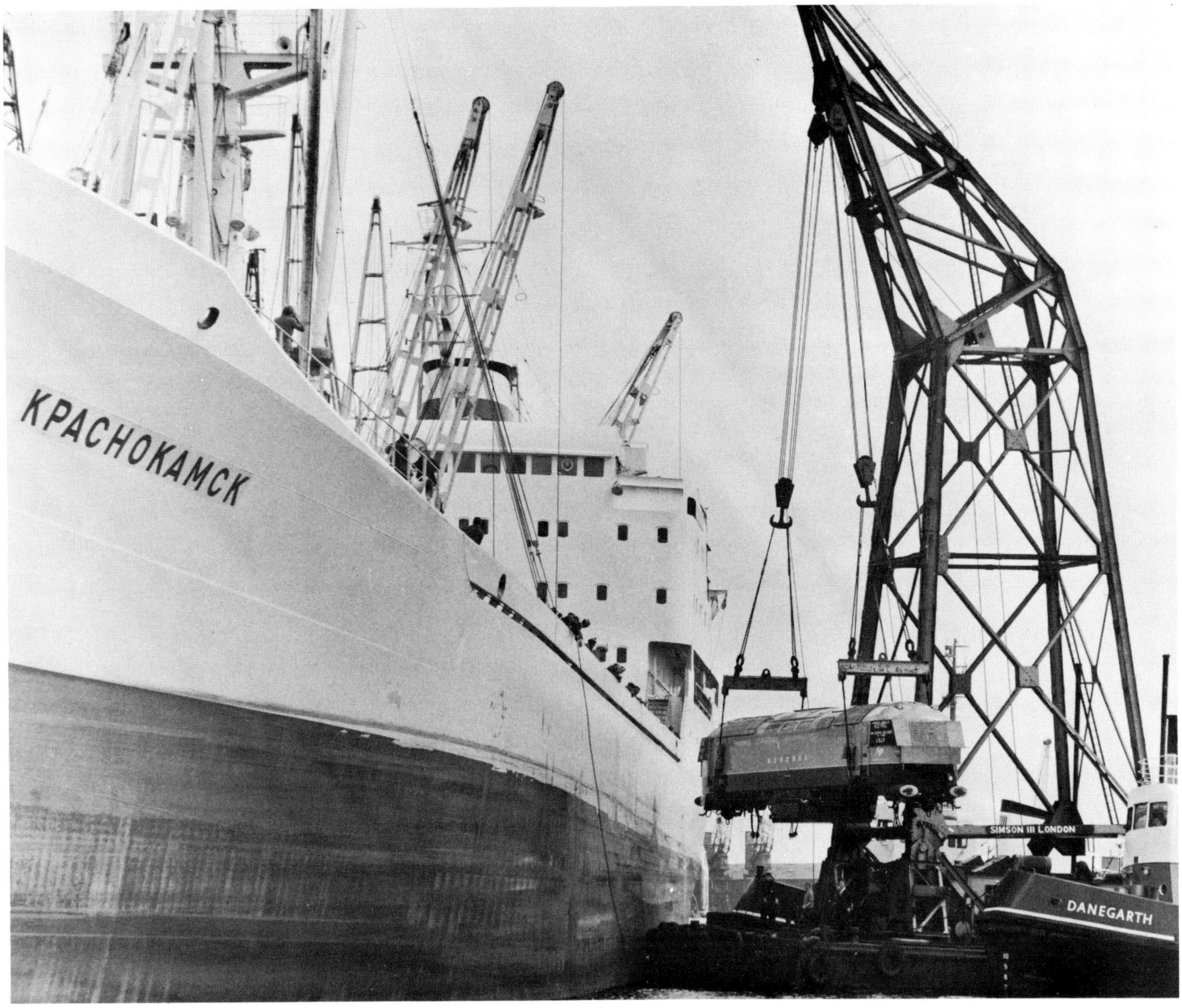
КРАСНОКАМСК
SIMSON III LONDON
DANEGARTH

3S74
HAWKER SIDDELEY
HS 4000

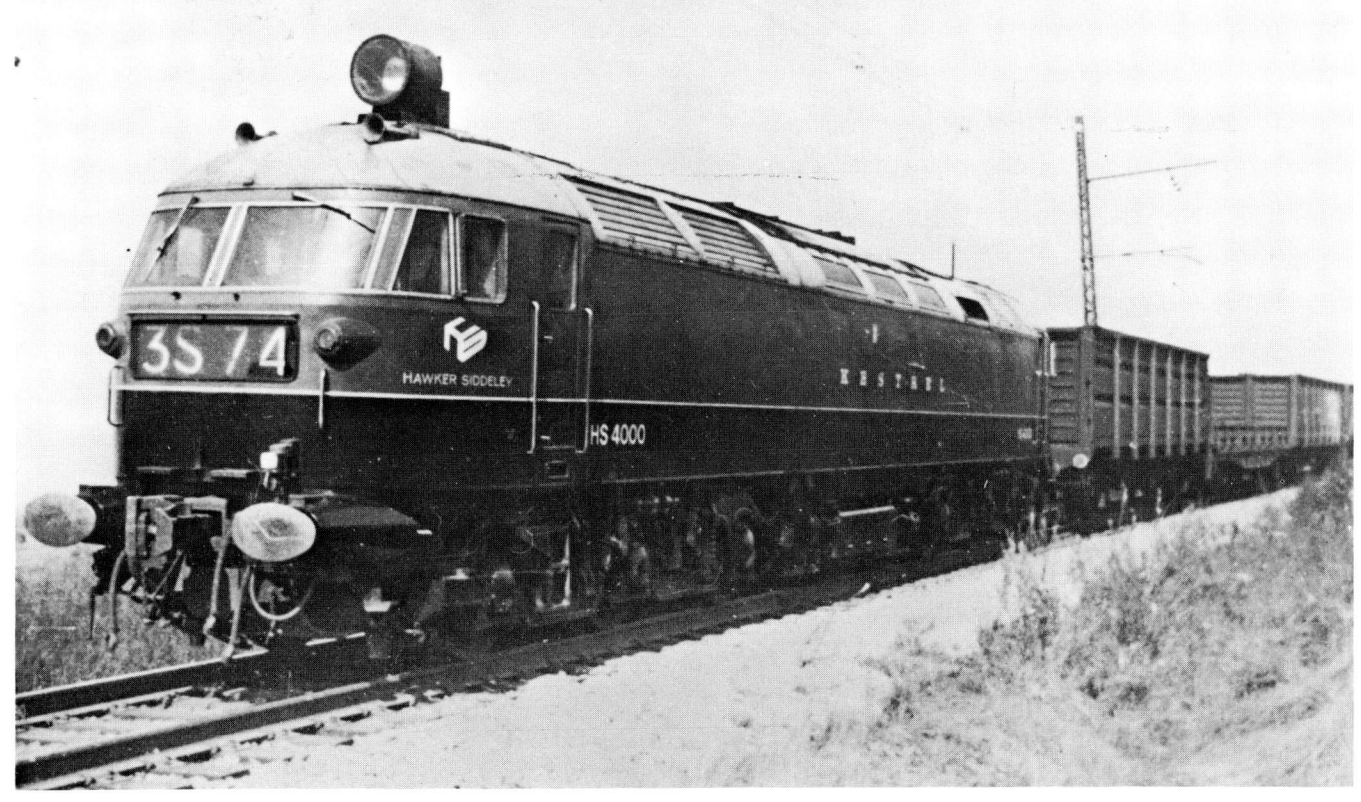

OVERSEAS AND INDUSTRIAL LOCOMOTIVES FROM 1962 ONWARDS

On 16 March 1962 Brush accepted delivery from Beyer-Peacock of an 0–6–0 diesel-electric shunter, rated at 400 bhp. It was powered by a National flat type engine and had a right angle drive gearbox between the traction motors and axles. The original idea was to provide an inexpensive alternative to the accepted method of drive prevalent at the time on diesel-electric shunters, i.e. nose-suspended axle-hung motors, with double-reduction geared drive. The traction motors in the latter condition were, and still are, mounted in line with the axles and although it was a well-proven method Brush explored the possibilities of using other arrangements that would still retain high tractive effort.

Externally the locomotive followed the lines previously set by the Brush-Beyer Peacock 0–4–0 shunters, except for the use of inside frames and a small bonnet behind the cab. The livery was the same orange and green scheme which had been used on the stock 0–4–0s of 1958, and the Beyer-Peacock works number was 7879, although no plate was ever carried. No Brush Traction number was ever allotted despite the fact that it was a Brush design. It would appear that it was the first of an intended batch of stock locomotives (Beyer 7879–83, Brush 104–8), but it is most likely that it remained the sole example of its type. Number 7879 saw very little service, and all of that was within the confines of the Falcon Works. It was not altogether a successful locomotive as there were frequent oil leaks from the fabricated gear case, and difficulty in negotiating the sharper curves on the works railway system. Added to these problems was the cessation of National engine production coupled with a fall in the demand for new shunting locomotives in Britain, due to British Railways disposing of many of their own redundant locomotives to industrial owners. Number 7879 was finally used for providing a load during Type 4 brake and wheelslip tests carried out on D1961 in 1967. Shortly afterwards it was moved and stored out of use on a short stub siding, which terminated at the base of Meadow Lane bridge. Its final setting here was one of being almost enveloped by the adjacent trees and bushes which have since taken over the site. In 1968 number 7879 was sold for scrap to Slag Reduction Ltd., of Rotherham, who presumably scrapped it without using it themselves.

117. In March 1962 Brush took delivery of a 0-6-0T built by Beyer Peacock as their No. 7879. A number of novel mechanical ideas was incorporated in the design, which was not a success and what little service the locomotive saw was entirely within Falcon Works. In 1968, after a life of only six years, it was sold for scrap. B.E.M.

On 8 September 1961 Rhodesian Railways placed an order with Brush for fourteen 1730 bhp Co-Co locomotives to deal with increasing traffic on their system. These units were intended to operate on the 257 mile route between Bulawayo and Malvernia, on the Rhodesia/Mozambique border. They were also the first locomotives to be built for the 3ft 6in gauge by Brush, the design being to a maximum axle load of 15 tons, and an overall weight of 90 tons in working order. They were classified DE 4 and numbered 1400 to 1413 (Brush 399–412) by Rhodesian Railways. The locomotives were also required to run in multiple with the English Electric Classes DE 2 (1200–34) and DE 3 (1300–15), thus ensuring good availability and versatility, whilst at the same time cutting down the numbers of footplatemen formerly required for steam haulage.

This was the second important export order for main line diesel-electric locomotives received by Brush, and indeed their ancestry could be traced back through the British Railways Type 2 to the original Ceylon locomotive order. It was mainly the influence of the highly successful Type 2 which led Rhodesia to seek locomotives from Brush in an effort to diversify their suppliers and not become too dependent on one particular builder. The order was based upon a hire-purchase arrangement, and English Electric also supplied locomotives during the same period to complete Rhodesian Railway's current requirements.

118. The 12-cylinder Mirrlees National diesel engine and Brush main generator being lowered into a Rhodesia Railways DE4 locomotive in the Turbine Shop in June 1963. B.E.M.

119. The first Rhodesia Railways DE4, No. 1400, stands completed on the mixed gauge track, at the back of the Falcon Works, on 12 September 1963. B.E.M.

Class DE 4s Leading Details were as follows:

Maximum Operating Speed	60 mph
Maximum Tractive Effort	57,800 lb
Continuous Tractive Effort at 13 mph	37,500 lb
Length over Buffer Beams	51ft 1in
Width over Framing	9ft 9in
Overall Height	13ft 4in
Bogie Wheelbase	13ft 0in
Bogie Pivot Centres	27ft 3in
Fuel Capacity	1000 gallons
Minimum Curve Negotiable	275ft 0in

In external appearance the locomotives bore a family resemblance to the Brush Type 4 and *Falcon*, particularly in the cab region and, like the former, all louvres and grilles were restricted to the roof area. The body was constructed on the integral pattern, which consisted basically of bodysides connected by cross-stretchers, deck plates and roof sections. At each end there were dragboxes fitted with a centre-buffing coupler, but no side buffers. The overall effect was quite pleasing, with green livery and cream lining applied to uncluttered bodysides, a far cry from the 'portholes' and grilles which were a feature of the Ceylon locomotives. For ease of maintenance there were two access doors, one each side, for removal of and access to small components, thus avoiding passage through the cabs. There were removable roof sections for access to all large equipment except the radiator section, which was load bearing. Whereas the main bodysides were of fabricated steel sheet, the cab sections consisted of aluminium and glass-fibre.

120. On 21 December 1963 Rhodesia Railways No. 1400 was moved to the dispatch siding. As the Rhodesian gauge is only 3ft 6in the locomotive had to be mounted on adaptor bogies for towing to the docks on the first stage of its journey to Africa.

B.E.M.

The bogies were cast steel 'Commonwealth' type with three Brush nose-suspended, force-ventilated traction motors fitted to each one. Unfortunately, in service the bogie frames have persistently cracked and strengthening ribs have had to be fitted. Also when the axles and traction motor suspension bearings became life-expired problems arose with non-availability of replacements, so new axles of modified design were introduced, incorporating standard bearings. The brakes on the locomotives were vacuum and air operated. The vacuum not only supplied the locomotive but also the train, although an independent air brake valve operated the locomotive brakes only.

The diesel engine fitted to the DE 4 Class was the Mirrlees National 12-cylinder, four-stroke, Vee-type, being pressure charged and inter-cooled. This engine was rated at 1920 bhp at 1000 rpm under normal conditions, but was only rated effectively at 1730 bhp in Rhodesia, through the prevailing operating conditions of 4,500 ft altitude, a temperature of 95°F, and a 50 per cent relative humidity. The engine and main generator were mounted on a common bedplate, the former having stress-relieved steel plate fabrications on the cylinder housing and upper crankcase parts. Cylinder liners were made from cast iron with continuous bore, enabling free downward expansion. In service, however, it was found that the fabricated steel crankcases were failing at the welds, particularly in the area of the camshaft bearing mounting pads through to the water space, and the eventual replacement of these crankcases by cast steel ones was effected by Rhodesian Railways, with Mirrlees supplying the parts. The foregoing troubles resulted in comparatively low mileages by the class, with some out of action for long periods under repair, while the rest were run below full rating when awaiting their turn for repair.

121. Rhodesia Railways No. 1407 awaits its next duty. Although signs of normal wear and tear are apparent, a very high standard of cleaning is maintained.   Rhodesia Railways.

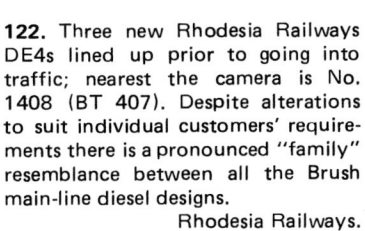

122. Three new Rhodesia Railways DE4s lined up prior to going into traffic; nearest the camera is No. 1408 (BT 407). Despite alterations to suit individual customers' requirements there is a pronounced "family" resemblance between all the Brush main-line diesel designs.
                    Rhodesia Railways.

123. Rhodesia Railways No. 1404 (BT 403) on a freight train in Rhodesia. Despite minor damage above the cow catcher, the high standard of external maintenance is very apparent.   Rhodesia Railways.

The main generator fitted was an 8-pole, compensated winding type rated at 1122 kW, 680v, 1650 amps and 1112 kW, 530v, 2100 amps, both ratings being continuous at 1000 rpm. The additional benefit of a series winding was included to facilitate engine starting from the batteries, which were situated below the deck and just above rail level.

Construction began in 1962 and the first one, number 1400, emerged during June 1963, having been constructed alongside the Type 4 production line. By the end of July No. 1400 had been tested, painted and was ready for the official handing-over ceremony. This took place on 9 August 1963, the locomotive being handed over by the Managing Director, Mr. M. C. Clear to Mr. A. M. Hawkins, the Assistant General Manager of Rhodesian Railways, who afterwards drove the locomotive along the works test track. Delivery from Loughborough commenced in December 1963 and 1400 entered Rhodesian Railways service on 22 April 1964. The final unit, 1413, entered service during January 1965.

124. The first of the DE4 Co-Cos supplied to Rhodesia Railways. When this photograph was taken No. 1400 was about to undertake a trial run, which accounts for all the people in the cab.   B.E.M.

It is almost certain that if Rhodesia had not declared itself independent and in consequence provoked international economic sanctions, Britain would have supplied more locomotives. In the event Rhodesia turned to the United States and was supplied by General Motors with nine 2090 bhp Co-Co single cab units of Class DE 6.

Facing page
125. A Rhodesia Railways freight train headed by two English Electric and one Brush locomotive. The resemblance of the former to the Peaks and the latter to the Type 2s is noticeable.
Rhodesia Railways.

Facing page
126. Rhodesia Railways No. 1407 (BT 406) piloting an English Electric diesel on a passenger train.   Rhodesia Railways.

The initial engine troubles mentioned earlier were overcome, and in service the locomotives proved to be capable and welcome additions to stock, but by the mid-seventies things had changed very much. During 1976 there were only three or four locomotives left in service, the remainder having had their duties taken over by new diesels. Leaks in various places caused the engine compartments to be covered in oil spray and many drivers would not enter the compartment during a run because of this. By 1977 the latest trouble was the badly worn crankshafts and most of the locomotives out of service required new ones, which were rumoured to be coming from South Africa. Whether or not they will all ever be returned to traffic remains uncertain, but possible political events which emerge in the future may affect policy and the uncertainty surrounding Class DE 4.

During 1963 representatives of Cuban National Railways visited Britain and discussed with British Railways which modern design of diesel locomotive could be adapted suitably to their requirements. Later that year it became known that the Brush Type 4 had been selected and that an order for ten locomotives had been placed with Clayton Equipment Company Ltd, which was to build them under licence at Hatton, near Derby. This seemingly devious method of obtaining locomotives was probably due to the prevailing political climate between Cuba and the United States at the time, and the possible adverse effects on Hawker Siddeley interests in North America should Brush have been the main contractor.

The general outline and appearance of the locomotives followed the Brush Type 4 very closely, with dragbox modifications to suit centre couplers and buffers. Additional equipment was a cab roof-mounted headlight, illuminated cab corner running numbers and roof-mounted warning horns. The livery ex-works was even in the Brush Type 4 two-tone style, with British Railways style numerals painted on the bodysides. Automatic air braking equipment only was fitted. The engine used was the French-built Sulzer 12-cylinder 12LVA 24 Vee-type, of 2534 bhp at 1050 rpm similar to those fitted experimentally to Class 48 locomotives D1702–6 in 1964/5.

127. The body shell of a Cuban Type 4, mounted on transporter bogies, seen on the Falcon Works test track on 11 December 1964.
B.E.M.

Main details were as follows:

Wheel Arrangement	Co-Co
Overall Length	64ft 0in
Distance between Bogie Centres	37ft 0in
Overall Height	13ft 0in
Maximum Speed	65 mph

Main d.c. Generator (Brush):
12 pole, 3-winding type, with one self-exciter, one separately excited and the third a series decompounding.

Continuous Rating	380v, 4260 amps at 1050 rpm
Maximum Rating	439v, 3720 amps at 1050 rpm
One Hour Rating	353v, 4570 amps at 1050 rpm

Brush Traction Motors (six):
Each 4-pole 336hp, nose-suspended, axle-hung force-ventilated type, 380v, 710amp rating at 693rpm

The body shells were manufactured at Loughborough, where some of the equipment was also installed, but final assembly and painting was done at the works of International Combustion Ltd., Derby, all movement being on adaptor bogies. Indeed, to facilitate the latter wooden-bodied wagons were adapted as match wagons. Trials were held on the Derby-Bristol route. Delivery of the ten locomotives, Cuban National Railways 2501–2510, but bearing no Brush plates, started in July 1965. The first two, 2501/2 were shipped from Hull on 30 July, 2503/4 on 2 September, 2505 on 18 October, 2506 on 26 October and the rest followed soon afterwards, delivery being completed early in 1966.

These ten Clayton locomotives caused some adjustments to be made to the Type 4 production lines at Loughborough. The construction of D1842–61 (intended to be Brush 604–23) was diverted from Falcon Works to Beyer-Peacock at Gorton, but in the event was undertaken by British Railways at Crewe. This gave Brush the time and space to help Clayton's by undertaking the necessary redesign work and initial construction of the Cuban locomotives. This also explains the later re-use of Brush numbers 604–623 on the Skopje shunters and the last B.R. Type 4s built at Loughborough.

Very little information from Cuba has emerged over the years since 1966, but it would appear that most of the class has been out of service for lengthy periods. This is mainly due to a lack of hard currency to buy spare engine parts and a measure of cannibalisation to keep the others running. Observers have noted that these locomotives have influenced Russian engineers, who have had close ties with Cuba since 1962, to incorporate Brush body design features in Russian-built locomotives. Russia has offered its 3000 hp version of the Cuban Type 4 for export, production being mainly directed to East Germany, in the form of Class 130, with a total of 102 units supplied. From Class 130 and *Kestrel* was developed the 4000 hp Class 131 freight locomotive, and in 1973 the standard Class 132 mixed duty locomotive, mentioned at the end of Chapter 7.

128. The Sulzer 2500 h.p. engine and Brush main generator are lowered into the body of one of the Cuban Type 4s, at the Hatton works of Clayton Equipment Company Ltd, during January 1966.
B.E.M.

129. An official works photograph of one of the Co-Cos supplied to Cuban National Railways in 1965/66 by Clayton Equipment Company Ltd. Brush supplied the electrical equipment and the body shell.
B.E.M.

130. The first of the ten Cuban Type 4s at the head of a freight train, soon after going into service on the island in 1966. B.E.M.

131. Cuban National Railways No. 2501 seen at an unidentified roundhouse on the island. The original British Railways style livery has given way to a more distinctive local design. B.E.M.

During June 1963 six standard-gauge 0–4–0 diesel-electric shunters, of basically Brush-Beyer Peacock design, were ordered for the Skopje Steelworks in Jugoslavia. They were built by Beyer Peacock, with Brush electrical equipment, but had Cummins NT 335 engines, rated at 275 bhp at 1900 rpm. These engines were similar to those fitted in some of Skopje Steelworks' earthmoving equipment. Delivery, during May 1964, was by sea, via Birkenhead, then overland from Thessoloniki, in Greece. They were put to work on heavy ore trains within the works complex, sometimes in pairs, as four of them had been fitted for working in tandem, being equipped with train air braking too. These locomotives were Brush 604–609, but none carried running numbers as far as can be ascertained. Incidentally, these were the last 0–4–0 diesel-electrics to emerge from Beyer Peacock's works, which closed down during 1965. Two of these locomotives (604/5) were formerly Brush 99 and 103, of the original stock batch of shunters, built in 1958 as already recorded. The six locomotives are still in service, and although news hardly ever comes out of Jugoslavia, the only troubles believed to have occurred arose during the overland delivery journey, when they were towed by rail and suffered hot axleboxes, by being continuously run too far in one direction.

132. One of the Brush-Beyer Peacock standard gauge 0-4-0 shunters for the Skopje Steelworks in Jugoslavia being lowered into the hold of the S.S. *Brescia* at Birkenhead Docks on 15 May 1965, for shipment to Thessaloniki.   B.E.M.

133. A pair of Brush-Beyer Peacock 0-4-0s operating in tandem on a train of hopper wagons at Skopje Steelworks in 1965. The superb state of the track is particularly striking, especially when compared with every other industrial and overseas location photograph in this book. B.E.M.

134. One of the six Brush-Beyer Peacock 0-4-0s supplied to Skopje Steelworks seen there at the head of a ballast train. B.E.M.

By 1965 it had become apparent that Brush would soon have to win the main part of its locomotive business from overseas sources against the full weight of international competition, the remaining portion coming from British industrial users, as British Railways could be expected to complete its dieselisation programme within a further two years. A range of diesel-electric locomotives was advertised as being avilable for use at home or abroad, particularly the latter, to be built by Brush, or under licence elsewhere. The engines available were either Cummins, up to 800 bhp or Caterpillar, up to 1050 bhp and 1500 bhp with speeds of 1350 rpm on the latter. These engines had originated in heavy commercial and earth-moving units and were also backed up by a world-wide spares organisation of long standing, so there were running and repair cost

savings to be made by potential customers. Traditional engines were available for applications above 1500 bhp. The types promoted were:

FS1 0–6–0 Shunters, rated at 650 bhp, the first of which were built in 1967/8 by the Australian Tulloch Company for Western Australian Government Railways.

S1/B B-B Locomotives of 1050 bhp (for Panay Island Railway, Philippines) and 720 bhp (for Cuban Sugar Railways).

S2/FB Co-Co Locomotives of 1500–2000 bhp (Rhodesia Railways type).

S3/FB Co-Co Locomotives of 2000–3000 bhp (Cuban Type 4 pattern).

S4/FB Locomotives of 4000 bhp of the *Kestrel* type.

In general terms the S1 locomotives were offered as inexpensive narrow gauge units for overseas service. This type was intended primarily for countries with external political problems and very slender financial resources, which very often had railway systems operating under difficult conditions too. Although the FS1 range never received a Loughborough order before the end of the sixties, the S1 range actually received three, one from Panay and two from the Cuban Sugar Railways. The Panay Island Railway was owned by the Development Bank of the Philippines which ordered on the railway's behalf one S1 type B-B locomotive on 24 May 1967. It was a 1050 bhp example, which was allotted running number 106 (Brush 719).

The main details were:

Engine	Caterpillar D398B, 1050 bhp at 1300 rpm
Main Generator	Brush compound-wound type, with separately-excited and self-excited fields, and a series winding for motoring to start engine.
Braking System	Compressed air.
Maximum Speed	50 mph
Track Gauge	3ft 6in
Width Overall	8ft 6½in
Length over Buffer Beams	35ft 0in
Total Wheelbase	25ft 6in
Maximum Height	12ft 3in
Wheel Diameter	2ft 9in
Minimum Radius Curve	100ft 0in
Fuel Capacity	500 gallons
Total Weight in Working Order	48 tons
Maximum Axle Load	12 tons

135. One of the S1 type B-B locomotives takes shape in the Super-structure Shop, during October 1967. B.E.M.

136. Two S1 B-B locomotives built for different owners in 1968. Nearer the camera is Brush Traction No. 719 for the Panay Island Railway (No. 106); in the background is one of the ones supplied to the Cuban Sugar Railways. Notice the different track gauges available in the Erecting Shop. B.E.M.

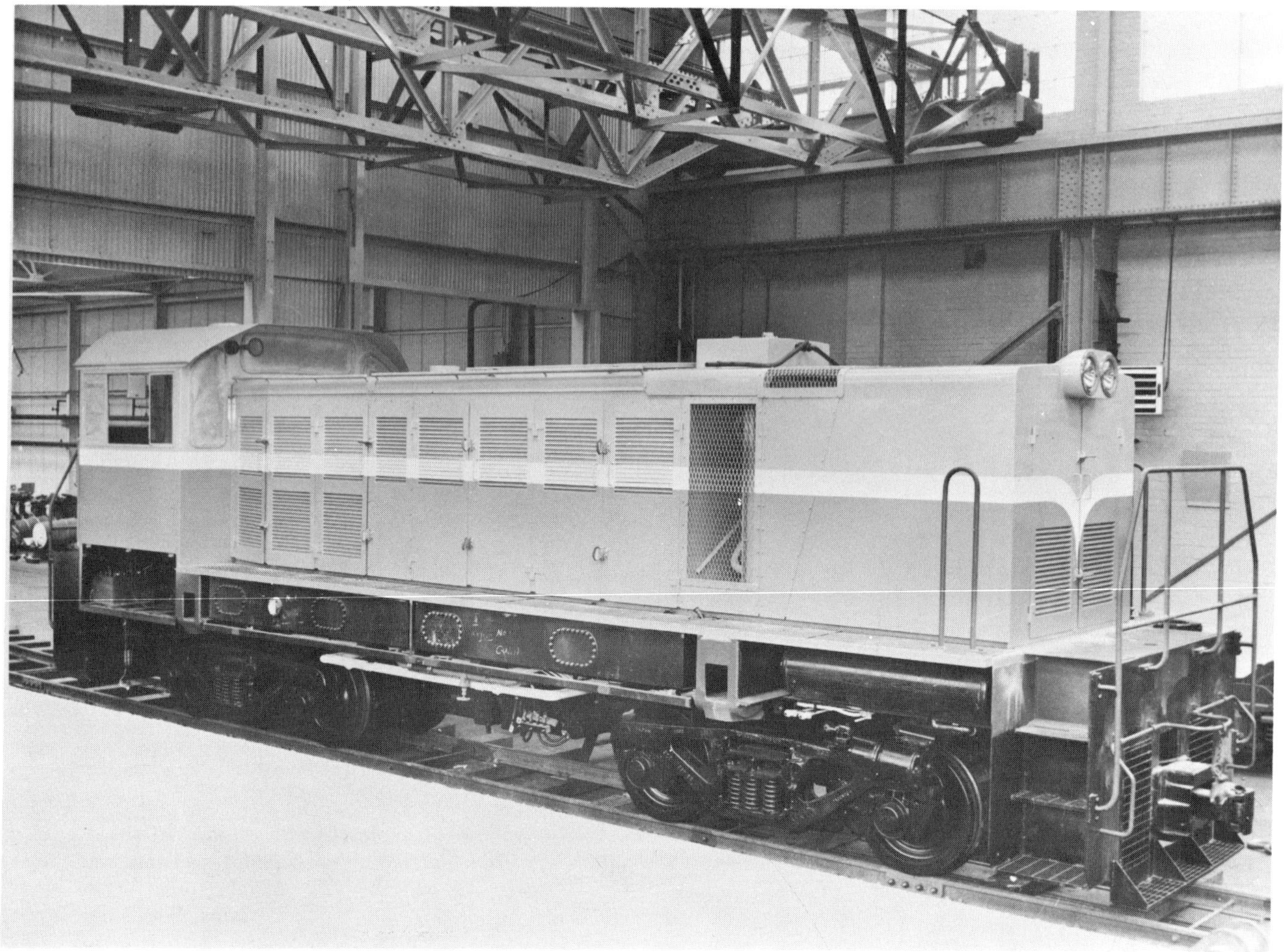

138. One of the S1 locomotives for Cuba mounted on road bogies for transit to the docks, on 18 April 1968. B.E.M.

The S1 units were light, inexpensive, narrow-gauge locomotives, aimed at potentially promising markets and the mode of construction bore the former point out, with much fabrication and a generally angular appearance. The frame was an all-welded structure, made up of two longitudinal channel sections, braced with cross members at the load bearing points, and at each end there was a box section housing the coupling and buffer beam. The bonnet doors were of the lift-off type, mounted upon pin hinges for ease of maintenance. There was a large spacious cab, with rear entrance door, situated at one end and a running board round the bonnet, with access from the cab front. Perhaps the most interesting departure from accepted Brush practice was the final drive arrangement, for although electric traction motors were used they were not mounted on the bogies, but on the underframes instead. They were three-point mounted, centrally and under the deck, between the bogies and were highly accessible. The motors were series wound, connected in parallel and force ventilated. The drive from each motor to its respective bogie was through a Cardan shaft to one axle, with an interconnecting shaft to a secondary gearbox on the other axle. The advantage of this arrangement in maintenance terms meant that no inspection pits were required for traction motor renewal, or inspection, and a comparatively short bogie could be employed. The S1 type locomotive was intended for light passenger, freight and shunting duties.

The Panay Island locomotive was built late in 1967 and completed during March 1968, being shipped from Royal Albert Dock, London on a Belships vessel during April. Perhaps the exceptionally poor financial situation and general decay of the railway made the chances of repeat orders unlikely, for 106 was the sole example ordered for it. The locomotive was reported still in service during 1977, running on the Phividec Railway. At the same time as 106 was being built, seven more S1 type B-B locomotives were being built for Cuban Sugar Railways (Minaz) too. These seven locomotives (Brush 712–718) were ordered on 15 April 1967, and were of a similar pattern to 106, but of 3ft gauge, and fitted with Paxman 720 bhp type 12 YH XL engines. No running numbers were allotted at the time of delivery, in 1968. A second order from Cuban Sugar Railways was placed on 4 July 1968, for a further eight locomotives, these being Brush 720 to 727.

139. Dwarfed by dockside cranes and the ship, Panay Island Railway No. 106 is lifted aboard by the ship's high-capacity derrick, ready for its long sea journey. B.E.M.

140. Panay Island Railway No. 106 heads a freight train through a country area. Notice the very inferior track and its poor state of maintenance. B.E.M.

Delivery of these S1s covered the period from December 1968 to 1969. The careers of these fifteen locomotives are somewhat obscure, a common occurrence in Communist countries, but it is believed that only a few were still in service by 1976, as very poor track conditions caused frequent mechanical failures in the transmission. Reports also suggest that the general policy in recent years has been towards the use of Russian equipment and a corresponding alteration of track gauge. A combination of these events probably brought about their demise, despite the fact that Brush engineers overcame the mechanical failures. After the last S1 locomotive was dispatched to Cuba there was a gradual run down of locomotive building activities. A lack of orders hit not only Brush, but several other well known companies too. At home the main line diesel programme was complete and the home industrial potential faded when British Railways sold off hundreds of comparatively modern redundant shunters to industry, due to a change of policy in freight train operation reducing shunting operations drastically. Abroad, it would seem that established foreign competition, particularly the American giant General Motors, had already pushed British locomotive builders out of most of their traditional markets.

Brush began to use the erecting shops for other purposes, and by 1970 had disposed of the works shunters and taken up some of the easily removable works track. Brush Traction started to concentrate on supplying electrical equipment to overseas railways, British Rail and locomotive builders, such as Hunslet, which did not normally use electric transmission for their standard locomotives. Brush also supplied electrical equipment for British Rail's 'High Speed Train'.

The first return to diesel construction came in 1972 when the Nigerian Railway Corporation ordered twenty-two 400 bhp 0–6–0 type FS1 diesel-electric shunters. This order was placed on 6 November, through the Crown Agents, and it came at a time when gas turbine alternator business had declined, thus leaving sufficient workshop space to build some locomotives

in one of the shops formerly used for erecting locomotives. It was thus once again possible to build some locomotives at Loughborough, rather than by subcontract at other manufacturers' works. The works numbers for these 0–6–0s were 728–749, and the Nigerian running numbers 921–942. The main details were as follows:

Engine	Ruston-Paxman 8 RPHXL Mk 7
Maximum Rating	400 bhp at 1250 rpm
Continuous Rating	364 bhp
Track Gauge	3ft 6in
Axle Load	13.5 tons
Weight in Full Working Order	39.5 tons
Width Overall	9ft 8in
Length over Buffer Beams	24ft 0in
Total Wheelbase Length	10ft 0in
Maximum Height	13ft 0in
Wheel Diameter	3ft 6¾in
Minimum Curve Radius	130ft
Fuel Capacity	400 gallons
Locomotive Speed	15 mph

The frames were made up from steel plate, and welded to a plate deck, resulting in an extremely robust structure, able to withstand shunting shocks. The cab was situated between two bonnets of unequal length, a short one containing the fuel tank, and a longer one housing the power unit and associated equipment. Lift-off pin-hinged access doors were fitted to the engine compartment. Brake equipment was air for the locomotive and vacuum for the train.

The main d.c. generator was a 3-field type with separately-excited, self-excited and series windings, the latter for use on engine starting from the batteries. The continuous ratings were:
235 kW, 178v, 1320 amps at 1250 rpm
240 kW, 250v, 960 amps at 1250 rpm
There were two 126 hp series-wound, nose-suspended, axle-hung, force-ventilated traction motors.

Externally the locomotives were impressive units, painted dark green, with a broad, horizontal yellow band around the bonnet sides and ends. The buffer beams were picked out in yellow and black stripes, in inverted vee form while the side rods and balance weights were red. Stainless steel numerals were used for the running numbers, fixed to the cab sides on a level with the Nigerian Railways shield emblem, applied in transfer form. The running numbers also appeared on the buffer beams in gold, black-shaded transfer form.

Before despatch the locomotives were tested on the new and short-lived test track within the works between the erecting bay, car park and test house. Delivery took place between June 1973 and March 1974.

On 16 August 1973 a commissioning ceremony was held at Lagos with officials of the Nigerian Railway Corporation and Brush representatives Mr. J. M. Durber and Mr. D. R. Minkley present. After the initial speeches Dr. R. A. B. Dikko, Federal Commissioner for Transport performed the ceremony and this was followed by a parade of four locomotives on three parallel tracks. After completion of deliveries the locomotives were allocated to three major depots Ebute Metta, Zaria and Kafanchan, but minor examinations were carried out at smaller depots, from where the locomotives worked for 30 day periods. They have proved to be reliable units and in consequence are well liked. In 1975 trials were conducted to test their suitability for main line duties, hauling up to 260 tons. This necessitated the removal of the maximum speed control device, which limited speeds to a maximum of 40 mph.

The success of these locomotives in service led to another order for twenty more units which was placed during April 1975, but delays in the order actually being placed resulted in another period when no locomotives were being constructed. Once more the production of traction equipment for railways carried on apace, indeed it has proved to be the mainstay of the business.

141. The first of a batch of twenty-two FS1 type 0-6-0 shunters ordered by the Nigerian Railway Corporation poses on the temporary 3ft 6in gauge works track for its official photograph in the summer of 1973. B.E.M.

EVENTS FROM 1974 ONWARDS

The year 1974 brought changes for Brush in the shape of the 3250 bhp heavy freight locomotives ordered by British Rail. The order was for thirty locomotives and was valued at £8.4 million. It represented the second stage of the Railways' policy, initiated back in 1968, not to build further mixed traffic locomotives, but to separate the two functions of passenger and freight duties. The first stage resulted in 1976 in the introduction on Western Region of the Class 252 high speed trains, the power cars of which were equipped with Brush a.c. generators and d.c. traction motors.

The new freight locomotive was designated Class 56 and, in addition to the thirty units from Brush, thirty were ordered from British Rail Workshops, Doncaster. All the locomotives were equipped electrically with Brush a.c. main generators, d.c. traction motors, control gear and electronics. The Company was not in a position to build locomotives of this size and quantity within the required period, so construction was subcontracted to Electroputere, whose works are at Craiova, in Romania. The basic reasons for choosing Romania were quick delivery, capacity and an out-of-balance Anglo-Romanian trade exchange in Britain's favour. The main details of Class 56 were:

Wheel Arrangement	Co-Co
Engine	General Electric Co. 'English Electric' 16-cylinder type 16 RK 3CT.
Continuous Rating	3520 bhp at 900 rpm
Maximum Speed	80 mph
Length over Buffers	63ft 6in
Total Wheelbase	47ft 10in
Distance between Bogie Centres	37ft 8in
Maximum Height	12ft 9⅜in
Maximum Width	9ft 2in
Wheel Diameter	3ft 9in
Minimum Curve Radius	3½ chains
Weight in Full Working Order	126 tons
Maximum Axle Load	21 tons
Fuel Capacity	1150 gallons

The main body structure followed the example of the Brush Type 4 by using an all-welded, stressed skin, monocoque assembly to reduce weight and be load-bearing. The cabs also followed the Type 4 pattern with the addition of unsightly jumper cable and attachments, but without route indicator panel and roof-mounted grille.

The obvious choice of engine was the English Electric Vee-type 16 RK 3CT MkIII, which developed 3520 bhp at 900 rpm, but was set at 3250 bhp in the Class 56. It incorporated intercooling and turbo-charging, and was a direct descendant of the engines fitted to the London Midland & Scottish Railway's diesel-electrics 10000/1 in 1947/8. Directly coupled to this fine engine was a Brush 12-pole, 3-phase a.c. main generator. It was combined with an auxiliary a.c. generator of the same type, for supplying air conditioning equipment, traction motor blowers, compressors and batteries. Each generator was of the now standard application brushless type, incorporating a rotating diode assembly for its own rectified excitation supply. The six d.c. traction motors were series wound, force-ventilated, axle-hung and nose-suspended, all being connected in series-parallel. Continuous rating of each motor was 344 kW, 420v, 910 amps at 620 rpm.

The bogie was of Swiss design, one used extensively in Romania and readily available, whereas the Class 47 bogie was not. It was of welded-frame construction, with cylindrical axle box guides bolted to the frame, the weight being carried by helical springs supported by equalisers pivoted on the axlebox undersides. Secondary suspension was by six coil springs. Brakes were clasp type, acting on all wheels, with independent air braking on the locomotive and proportional control automatic train braking.

Construction commenced in 1975, with most of the equipment being sent from Britain to Romania for installation; Doncaster Works also started construction, but a little later. By April 1976 the first locomotive, numbered 56.001, had been built, and was undergoing trials in the Craiova area of Romania.

The locomotives ordered in 1974 were 56.001–30 (Brush 750–779) and 56.031–60 (Doncaster).

On 4 August 1976 56.001/2 were handed over at Zeebrugge, after their rail journey across Europe, and were loaded onto the ferry for Harwich. They remained at Harwich until 7 August when a Brush Type 2 towed them dead through Colchester, Ipswich and March to Tinsley depot, Sheffield. Most of the other locomotives followed this pattern of delivery from Harwich, to be received by Brush engineers at Tinsley. Indeed, it was expected that once accepted by British Railways they would be allocated to Tinsley for intensive diagrams on Merry-go-round trains between collieries and power stations. It was the sudden turn-round in Government policy after the 1973 oil crisis which rekindled interest in increased coal production for electricity generation, instead of oil. This in turn prompted the need for Class 56 and its short term delivery. Unfortunately, teething problems so beset the Romanian locomotives that the quick delivery was completely offset, which in turn delayed the Railways' acceptance of the first units until March 1977.

142. The first of the Romanian-built Class 56 heavy freight locomotives stands outside the Electroputere works at Craiova, in April 1976. Delivery was by rail to Zeebrugge, then by train ferry to Harwich. B.E.M.

143. Typical panel transfers of Class 56 locomotives, as seen on 56.003 at Shirebrook on 22 January 1978. D. Hawkins.

144. Head-on view of 56.010 at Shirebrook depot on 22 January 1978. D. Hawkins.

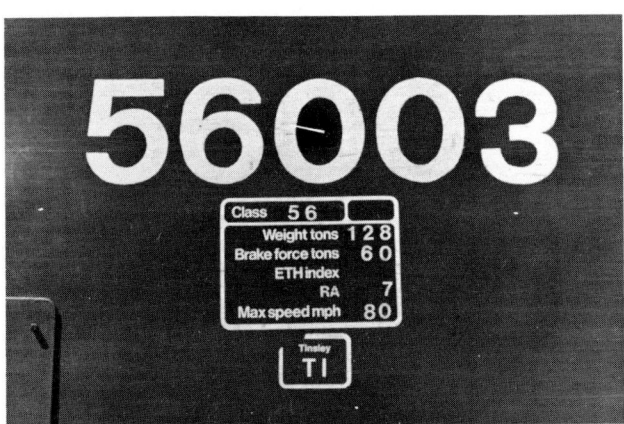

It is too recent history to comment at length on this period, but initial trials were held on the Settle-Carlisle route, and much time was spent by Brush engineers correcting faults and bringing the locomotives up to the required standards. On 1–2 November 1976 56.005 was exhibited in unfinished condition at Loughborough Midland Station, in conjunction with the visit of the Institution of Mechanical Engineers (Railway Division) to the Falcon Works. By the end of 1976 it seemed likely that British Rail would build thirty more Class 56 (56.061–90), for delivery in late 1978, to be followed by a further thirty locomotives a year to replace older diesel-electrics. Indeed, in 1977 British Rail were believed to be tendering for eighty more locomotives (56.091–170) and a new era on the Railway was under way.

145. Three Class 56s (56.017, 56.027 and 56.012) stand at Shire-brook diesel depot on 4 April 1978, awaiting turns of duty.

D. Hawkins.

146. A Resita worksplate of the type fitted to the bogies of Romanian-built Class 56 locomotives.

D. Hawkins.

147. No. 56.027 running light engine at Warsop Junction on 4 April 1978.

D. Hawkins.

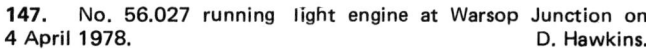

148. A line-up of Brush locomotives at Shirebrook depot on 22 January 1978. From left to right are: 56.027, 31.235 (D 5662) and 47.169 (D 1764). D. Hawkins.

149. No. 56.017 seen shortly after leaving Shirebrook depot on 4 April 1978. D. Hawkins.

During April 1976, Brush received another locomotive order, valued at £3.5 million, for twenty more FS1 0–6–0 shunters, for the Nigerian Railway Corporation. The order had long been anticipated and this date really marked the formal signing of the contract because material orders had already taken place. The order was for units basically identical to the first order of 22, but this time a top speed of 30 mph was specified as a result of the trials mentioned in Chapter 8. These locomotives were initially 943–962 (Brush 780–799), but the series was altered in December 1976 when the Crown Agents informed Brush that they must be numbered 951–970, as the Nigerian Railways numbered their batches from xx1 onwards for each batch.

The frame of the first locomotive was completed and despatched to the Turbine Shop for fitting out and erection in August 1976. It was tested during the latter part of January 1977, and spent almost a month being lavishly prepared for final painting, before emerging complete and ready for dispatch early in March. On 10 March 1977, 951 left Falcon Works on a low loader lorry bound for Liverpool Docks and shipment to Apapa. Deliveries continued at an average of two a month during 1977. A further order for an FS1 locomotive, identical to the Nigerian units, was placed during June 1976 by Ashaka Cement Company of Nigeria, a member of the Blue Circle Cement Group. Some indecision as to its numbering occurred, first being allocated Ashaka number 01, then 201, and finally 001. Brush

number 800 was allocated on 27 January, 1977. The locomotive was originally built as the fifth unit for Nigeria but during mid-March it was diverted to the new contract, just before the test and paint stage. The latter process resulted in an overall rich blue livery, with the running numbers and Ashaka Cement emblem applied in transfer form, in orange. The locomotive left Falcon Works on 24 May 1977.

During mid-December 1976, Tyne & Wear Passenger Transit ordered four FS1 0–6–0 diesel-electric shunters. These were for use on the electrified Metro system under construction at the time, but intended specifically for maintenance train haulage during de-energised periods. During September 1977 running numbers WL1–4 (Brush 801–804) were allocated. The main features were cut-down mountings, particularly the cab, and the fitting of a Rolls-Royce engine. One departure from previous practice was the use of a single traction motor, driving the centre axle. Assembly of the first locomotive commenced in August 1977.

At the time of writing (September 1977) the future looks promising for erecting shunting locomotives at the Falcon Works, thus continuing a tradition founded by Henry Hughes, way back in 1865.

150. Gleaming in its bright yellow livery, the first of the four FS1 shunters for the Tyne & Wear Metro stands in the former Turbine Shop, awaiting dispatch. Note the dual couplings and low-profile cab. Despite being delivered in January 1978, WL1 was Brush 801 of 1977.   B.E.M.

151. The Falcon Works in 1963 at the onset of Type 4 production, looking north-west. Bottom left can be seen Type 4's awaiting delivery, painting and test with 0-6-0 and 0-4-0 works shunters in attendance. Access to the Midland was to the rear of the station, lower left in the photograph.

152. Another 1963 view of the Falcon Works, this time looking north-east. To the left of the tall pair of chimneys is the former Turbine shop. The test track can be seen clearly extending into the Loughborough Meadow between the new Traction superstructure shops and the Great Central embankment.

BR class 31 (Type 2)
re numbering

Brush No.	B.R. No.		Date to Traffic	Initial Allocation	Notes
71	5500	31.018	10/57	30A	Wdn. WE Aug 8 1976 Preserved by NRM York
72	5501	31.001	11/57	30A	Wdn. WE Aug 8 1976
73	5502	31.002	12/57	30A	
74	5503	31.003	1/58	30A	
75	5504	31.004	1/58	30A	
76	5505	31.005	2/58	30A	
77	5506	31.006	3/58	30A	
78	5507	31.007	4/58	30A	Wdn. WE Nov 7 1976
79	5508	31.008	4/58	30A	
80	5509	31.009	5/58	30A	Wdn. WE Aug 8 1976
81	5510	31.010	5/58	30A	Wdn. WE Aug 8 1976
82	5511	31.011	6/58	30A	Wdn. WE Aug 8 1976
83	5512	31.012	6/58	30A	Wdn. WE Nov 7 1976
84	5513	31.013	7/58	30A	
85	5514	31.014	7/58	30A	Wdn. WE Nov 7 1976
86	5515	31.015	7/58	30A	
87	5516	31.016	9/58	30A	Wdn. WE Aug 8 1976
88	5517	31.017	9/58	30A	
89	5518	31.101	10/58	30A	
90	5519	31.019	12/58	30A	
119	5520	31.102	2/59	30A	
120	5521	31.103	3/59	32B	
121	5522	31.418	3/59	30A	
122	5523	31.105	3/59	30A	
123	5524	31.106	3/59	30A	
124	5525	31.107	3/59	31B	
125	5526	31.108	4/59	30A	
126	5527	31.109	4/59	30A	
127	5528	31.110	4/59	32A	
128	5529	31.111	5/59	31B	
129	5530	31.112	5/59	31B	
130	5531	31.113	5/59	30A	
131	5532	31.114	6/59	32A	
132	5533	31.115	6/59	32A	
133	5534	31.116	6/59	31B	
134	5535	31.117	6/59	32A	
135	5536	31.118	6/59	30A	
136	5537	31.119	6/59	30A	
137	5538	31.120	7/59	32B	
138	5539	31.121	7/59	32B	
139	5540	31.122	7/59	32B	
140	5541	31.123	7/59	32B	
141	5542	31.124	7/59	32B	
142	5543	31.125	7/59	32B	
143	5544	31.126	8/59	32B	
144	5545	31.127	10/59	32B	
145	5546	31.128	8/59	32B	
146	5547	31.129	8/59	32B	
147	5548	31.130	9/59	32B	
148	5549	31.131	9/59	32B	
149	5550	31.132	9/59	32B	
150	5551	31.133	9/59	32B	
151	5552	31.134	9/59	32B	
152	5553	31.135	9/59	32B	
153	5554	31.136	10/59	32B	
154	5555	31.137	10/59	32B	
155	5556	31.138	10/59	32B	
156	5557	31.139	10/59	32B	
157	5558	31.140, 31.421	10/59	32B	
158	5559	31.141	10/59	32B	
159	5560	31.142	10/59	32B	
160	5561	31.143	10/59	32B	
161	5562	31.144	11/59	32B	
162	5563	31.145	11/59	31B	
163	5564	31.146	11/59	31B	
164	5565	31.147	11/59	31B	
165	5566	31.148	11/59	31A	
166	5567	31.149	11/59	34B	
167	5568	31.150	12/59	34B	Accident victim. Wdn. 10.75
168	5569	31.151	12/59	34B	
169	5570	31.152	12/59	31B	
170	5571	31.153	12/59	31B	
171	5572	31.154	12/59	31B	
172	5573	31.155	12/59	31B	
173	5574	31.156	12/59	32A	
174	5575	31.157, 31.424	12/59	32A	
175	5576	31.158	12/59	32A	
176	5577	31.159	12/59	32A	
177	5578	31.160	1/60	30A	
178	5579	31.161	1/60	30A	
180	5580	31.162	1/60	32A	
181	5581	31.163	1/60	32A	
182	5582	31.164	1/60	32A	
183	5583	31.165	1/60	30A	
184	5584	31.166	1/60	31B	
185	5585	31.167	1/60	31B	
186	5586	31.168	2/60	34B	
187	5587	31.169	2/60	34B	
188	5588	31.170	2/60	34B	
189	5589	31.401	2/60	34B	
190	5590	31.171	2/60	34B	
191	5591	31.172, 31.420	2/60	34B	
192	5592	31.402	2/60	34B	
193	5593	31.173	3/60	34B	
194	5594	31.174	3/60	34B	
195	5595	31.175	3/60	34B	
196	5596	31.403	3/60	34B	
197	5597	31.176	3/60	34B	
198	5598	31.177	3/60	34B	
199	5599	31.178	3/60	34B	
200	5600	31.179	3/60	34B	
201	5601	31.180	3/60	34B	
202	5602	31.181	3/60	34B	
203	5603	31.182	3/60	34B	
204	5604	31.183	4/60	34B	
305	5605	31.404	4/60	34B	
206	5606	31.405	4/60	34B	
207	5607	31.184	4/60	34B	
208	5608	31.185	4/60	34G	
209	5609	31.186	4/60	34B	
210	5610	31.187	4/60	34G	
211	5611	31.188	4/60	34G	
212	5612	31.189	5/60	34G	
213	5613	31.190	5/60	34G	
214	5614	31.191	5/60	34G	
215	5615	31.192	5/60	34G	
216	5616	31.406	5/60	30A	
217	5617	31.193	5/60	30A	
218	5618	31.194	5/60	30A	
219	5619	31.195	5/60	30A	
220	5620	31.196	6/60	31B	
221	5621	31.197, 31.423	6/60	31B	
222	5622	31.198	6/60	32B	
223	5623	31.199	6/60	32B	
224	5624	31.200	6/60	32B	
225	5625	31.201	6/60	32B	
226	5626	31.202	6/60	32B	
227	5627	31.203	6/60	32B	
228	5628	31.204	6/60	32A	
229	5629	31.205	6/60	32A	
230	5630	31.206	7/60	32A	
231	5631	31.207	7/60	32A	
232	5632	31.208	7/60	30A	
233	5633	31.209	7/60	30A	
234	5634	31.210	7/60	30A	
235	5635	31.211	7/60	30A	
236	5636	31.212	7/60	30A	
237	5637	31.213	7/60	30A	
238	5638	31.214	8/60	30A	
239	5639	31.215	8/60	34G	
240	5640	31.407	8/60	34G	
241	5641	31.216	8/60	34G	
242	5642	31.217	8/60	34G	
243	5643	31.218	8/60	34G	
244	5644	31.219	8/60	34G	

245	5645	31.220	9/60	34G
246	5646	31.408	9/60	34G
247	5647	31.221	9/60	34G
248	5648	31.222	9/60	34G
249	5649	31.223	9/60	34G
250	5650	31.224	9/60	34G
251	5651	31.225	9/60	34G
252	5652	31.226	9/60	34G
253	5653	31.227	9/60	34G
254	5654	31.228	9/60	34G
255	5655	31.229	9/60	31B
256	5656	31.409	10/60	31B
257	5657	31.230	10/60	31B
258	5658	31.231	10/60	31B
259	5659	31.232	10/60	31B
260	5660	31.233	10/60	31B
261	5661	31.234	10/60	31B
262	5662	31.235	10/60	31B
263	5663	31.236	11/60	31B
264	5664	31.237	11/60	31B
265	5665	31.238	11/60	31B
266	5666	31.239	11/60	31B
267	5667	31.240	11/60	31B
268	5668	31.241	11/60	31B
269	5669	31.410	11/60	31B
270	5670	31.242	1/61	31B
271	5671	31.243	10/60	41A
272	5672	31.244	11/60	34G
273	5673	31.245	12/60	34G
274	5674	31.246	12/60	34G
275	5675	31.247	12/60	34G
276	5676	31.248	12/60	34G
277	5677	31.249	12/60	34G
278	5678	31.250	12/60	34G
279	5679	31.251	12/60	34G
281	5680	31.252	12/60	41A
282	5681	31.253	1/61	41A
283	5682	31.254	1/61	41A
284	5683	31.255	1/61	41A
285	5684	31.256	1/61	41A
286	5685	31.257	2/61	41A
287	5686	31.258	2/61	41A
288	5687	31.259	2/61	41A
289	5688	31.260	2/61	41A
290	5689	31.261	3/61	41A
291	5690	31.262	3/61	41A
292	5691	31.411	3/61	41A
293	5692	31.412	3/61	41A
294	5693	31.263	3/61	41A
295	5694	31.264	4/61	30A
296	5695	31.265	4/61	30A
297	5696	31.266	5/61	30A
298	5697	(31.267)	5/61	30A
		31.419		
299	5698	31.268	5/61	30A
300	5699	31.269	4/61	30A
301	5800	31.270	6/61	31B
302	5801	31.271	6/61	30A
303	5802	31.272	6/61	31B
304	5803	31.273	6/61	31B
305	5804	31.274	6/61	41A
306	5805	31.275	7/61	41A
307	5806	31.276	7/61	41A
308	5807	31.277	7/61	41A
309	5808	31.278	7/61	41A
310	5809	31.279	7/61	41A
311	5810	31.280	8/61	41A
312	5811	31.281	8/61	41A
313	5812	31.413	8/61	41A
314	5813	31.282	9/61	41A
315	5814	31.414	9/61	41A
316	5815	31.283	9/61	41A
317	5816	31.284	9/61	41A
318	5817	31.285	10/61	41A
319	5818	31.286	10/61	41A
320	5819	31.287	10/61	41A

321	5820	31.288	10/61	41A
322	5821	31.289	11/61	41A
323	5822	31.290	11/61	41A
324	5823	31.291	11/61	41A
325	5824	31.415	11/61	41A
326	5825	31.292	11/61	41A
362	5826	31.293	12/61	41A
363	5827	31.294	12/61	41A
364	5828	31.295	12/61	41A
365	5829	31.296	1/62	41A
366	5830	31.297	1/62	41A
367	5831	31.298	1/62	41A
368	5832	31.299	2/62	41A
369	5833	31.300	2/62	41A
370	5834	31.301	3/62	41A
371	5835	31.302	4/62	41A
372	5836	31.303	4/62	41A
373	5837	31.304	4/62	41A
374	5838	31.305	4/62	41A
375	5839	31.306	5/62	41A
376	5840	31.307	5/62	41A
377	5841	31.308	5/62	41A
378	5842	31.416	5/62	41A
379	5843	31.309	5/62	41A
380	5844	31.310,	6/62	41A
		31.422		
381	5845	31.311	6/62	41A
382	5846	31.312	6/62	41A
383	5847	31.313	6/62	41A
384	5848	31.314	7/62	41A
385	5849	31.315	7/62	41A
386	5850	31.316	7/62	41A
387	5851	31.317	7/62	41A
388	5852	31.318	8/62	41A
389	5853	31.319	8/62	30A
390	5854	31.320	8/62	30A
391	5855	31.321	8/62	31B
392	5856	31.417	8/62	31B
393	5857	31.322	9/62	41A
394	5858	31.323	9/62	41A
395	5859	31.324	10/62	41A
396	5860	31.325	10/62	41A
397	5861	31.326	10/62	41A
398	5862	31.327	10/62	41A

N.B. The Works Numbers of 5697/8/9 may have been transposed as 299/300/298, at Loughborough. Also 5834 was plated no. 371.

Locomotive Depot Codes

30A	Stratford
31B	March
32A	Norwich
32B	Ipswich
34B	Hornsey
41A	Tinsley

BR class 47 (Type 4) re numbering

Brush No.	BR No.	Date to Traffic	Initial Allocation	Notes
342	1500 47.401	11/62	34G	
343	1501 47.402	11/62	34G	
344	1502 47.403	11/62	34G	
345	1503 47.404	12/62	34G	
346	1504 47.405	1/63	34G	
347	1505 47.406	1/63	34G	
348	1506 47.407	1/63	34G	
349	1507 47.408	1/63	34G	
350	1508 47.409	1/63	34G	
351	1509 47.410	2/63	34G	
352	1510 47.411	2/63	34G	
353	1511 47.412	2/63	34G	
354	1512 47.413	3/63	34G	
355	1513 47.414	3/63	34G	
(356) 357	1514 47.415	3/63	34G	
(357) 356	1515 47.416	3/63	34G	
358	1516 47.417	4/63	34G	
359	1517 47.418	4/63	34G	
(360) 413	1518 47.419	5/63	34G	
(361) 360	1519 47.420	4/63	34G	
(413) 414	1520 47.421	6/63	34G	
(414) 415	1521 47.001	6/63	34G	
(415) 417	1522 47.002	6/63	34G	
416	1523 47.003	6/63	34G	
(417) 419	1524 47.004	6/63	34G	
418	1525 47.422	6/63	34G	
(419) 420	1526 47.005	6/63	34G	
(420) 421	1527 47.423	6/63	34G	
(421) 422	1528 47.006	6/63	34G	
(422) 423	1529 47.007	6/63	34G	
(423) 424	1530 47.008	6/63	34G	
(424) 425	1531 47.424	6/63	34G	
(425) 426	1532 47.009	6/63	34G	
(426) 427	1533 47.425	8/63	34G	
(427) 428	1534 47.426	8/63	41A	
(428) 429	1535 47.427	8/63	41A	
(429) 430	1536 47.428	8/63	41A	
(430) 431	1537 47.010	8/63	41A	
(431) 432	1538 47.011	9/63	41A	
(432) 433	1539 47.012	9/63	41A	
(433) 434	1540 47.013	9/63	41A	
(434) 436	1541 47.429	9/63	41A	
435	1542 47.430	9/63	41A	
(436) 438	1543 47.014	9/63	41A	
437	1544 47.015	10/63	41A	
(438) 439	1545 47.431	10/63	41A	
(439) 440	1546 47.016	10/63	41A-34G	
(440) 441	1547 47.432	10/63	34G	
(441) 442	1548 47.433	10/63	41A	
(442) 443	1549 47.434	10/63	41A	
444	1682 47.096	10/63	81A	
445	1683 47.485	10/63	81A	
446	1684 47.097	11/63	81A	
447	1685 47.098	11/63	2B	
448	1686 47.099	11/63	2B	
449	1687 47.100	11/63	2B	
450	1688 47.101	11/63	2B	
451	1689 47.486	11/63	82A	
452	1690 47.102	11/63	86A	
453	1691 47.103	11/63	86A	
454	1692 47.104	11/63	82A	
455	1693 47.105	12/63	82A	
456	1694 47.106	12/63	81A	
457	1695 47.107	12/63	2B-16C	
458	1696 47.108	12/63	16C	
(459) 460	1697 47.109	12/63	86A	
(460) 459	1698 47.110	1/64	81A	
461	1699 47.111	12/63	81A	
462	1700 47.112	1/64	81A	
463	1701 47.113	1/64	81A	
464	1702 47.114	11/65	41A	Works Insp. 7.64
465	1703 47.115	9/65	41A	Works Insp. 8.65
466	1704 47.116	7/66	41A	Works Insp. 7.64
467	1705 47.117	11/65	41A	Works Insp. 8.64
468	1706 47.118	12/65	41A	Works Insp. 8.64
469	1707 47.487	1/64	81A	
470	1708 47.119	1/64	81A	
471	1709 47.120	1/64	2B	
472	1710 47.121	1/64	81A	
473	1711 47.122	1/64	81A	
474	1712 47.123	1/64	2B	
475	1713 47.488	1/64	2B	
476	1714 47.124	2/64	81A	
477	1715 47.125 (47.548)	2/64	81A-2B	
(478) 487	1716 47.489	2/64	2B	
(479) 488	1717 47.126 47.555	2/64	81A	
(480) 489	1718 (47.127) 47.539	2/64	86A	
(481) 490	1719 47.128	2/64	86A	
(482) 491	1720 47.129	3/64	82A	
(483) 492	1721 47.130	3/64	87E	
(484) 493	1722 47.131	2/64	82A	
(485) 494	1723 (47.132) 47.540	3/64	82A	
(486) 495	1724 (47.133) 47.549	3/64	82A	
(487) 496	1725 47.490	3/64	82A	
(488) 497	1726 48.134	3/64	86A	
(489) 498	1727 47.135	4/64	81A	
(490) 499	1728 47.136	4/64	86A	
(491) 500	1729 47.137	4/64	87E	
(492) 501	1730 47.138	4/64	86A	
(493) 502	1731 (47.139) 47.550	6/64	86A	
(494) 503	1732 47.140	4/64	86A	
(495) 504	1733 47.141	6/64	81A	
(496) 505	1734	5/64	82A	(Accident Victim Wdn. 3/65)
(497) 506	1735 47.142	5/64	87E-86A	
(498) 508	1736 47.143	4/64	86A	
(499) 507	1737 47.144	5/64	86A	
(500) 509	1738 47.145	5/64	86A	
(501) 510	1739 47.146	6/64	87A-86A	
(502) 511	1740 47.147	6/64	81A	
(503) 512	1741 47.148	6/64	86A	
(504) 513	1742 47.149	5/64	86A	
(505) 514	1743 47.150	6/64	81A	
(506) 515	1744 47.151	6/64	86A	
(507) 516	1745 47.152	7/64	81A	
(508) 517	1746 47.153, 47.551	7/64	81A	
(509) 518	1747 (47.154) 47.546	7/64	81A	
(510) 519	1748 47.155	7/64	81A	
(511) 486	1749 47.156	7/64	82A	
(512) 478	1750 47.157	7/64	82A	
(513) 479	1751 47.158	7/64	87E	
(514) 480	1752 47.159	7/64	87E	
(515) 481	1753 47.491	7/64	2B	
(516) 482	1754 47.160	8/64	87E	
(517) 483	1755 (47.161) 47.541	8/64	87E	
(518) 484	1756 47.162	9/64	87E	
(519) 485	1757 47.163	9/64	86A	
520	1758 47.164	5/64	41A	
521	1759 47.165	8/64	41A	
522	1760 47.492	9/64	41A	
523	1761 47.166	9/64	41A	
524	1762 47.167	9/64	41A	
525	1763 47.168	9/64	41A	
526	1764 47.169	9/64	41A	
527	1765 47.170	9/64	41A	
528	1766 47.171	9/64	41A	
529	1767 47.172	10/64	41A	
530	1768 47.173	10/64	41A	
531	1769 47.174	10/64	41A	
532	1770 47.175	10/64	41A	
533	1771 47.176	10/64	41A	

534	1772	47.177	10/64	41A
535	1773	47.178	9/64	41A
536	1774	47.179	10/64	41A
537	1775	47.180	10/64	41A
538	1776	47.181	10/64	41A
539	1777	47.182	11/64	41A
540	1778	47.183	10/64	41A
541	1779	47.184	10/64	41A
542	1780	47.185	10/64	41A
543	1781	47.186	11/64	41A
544	1782	47.301	11/64	41A
545	1783	47.302	11/64	41A
546	1784	47.303	11/64	41A
547	1785	47.304	12/64	41A
548	1786	47.305	11/64	41A
549	1787	47.306	11/64	41A
550	1788	47.307	12/64	41A
551	1789	47.308	11/64	41A
552	1790	47.309	12/64	41A
553	1791	47.310	12/64	41A
554	1792	47.311	1/65	41A
555	1793	47.312	12/64	41A
556	1794	47.313	12/64	41A
557	1795	47.314	1/65	41A
558	1796	47.315	1/65	41A
559	1797	47.316	1/65	41A
560	1798	47.317	1/65	41A
561	1799	47.318	1/65	41A
562	1800	47.319	1/65	41A
563	1801	47.320	1/65	41A
564	1802	47.321	1/65	41A
565	1803	47.322	1/65	41A
566	1804	47.323	2/65	41A
567	1805	47.324	1/65	41A
568	1806	47.325	1/65	41A
569	1807	47.326	P1/65	D16
570	1808	47.327	P1/65	D16
571	1809	47.328	P1/65	D16
572	1810	47.329	P2/65	D16
573	1811	47.330	P2/65	D16
574	1812	47.331	P2/65	D16
575	1813	47.332	P2/65	D16-5A
576	1814	47.333	P2/65	D16
577	1815	47.334	P2/65	D16-5A
578	1816	47.335	P2/65	D16
579	1817	47.336	P3/65	D16
580	1818	47.337	P2/65	D16
581	1819	47.338	P2/65	D16
582	1820	47.339	P2/65	D16
583	1821	47.340	P3/65	D16
584	1822	47.341	P3/65	D16
585	1823	47.342	P3/65	D16
586	1824	47.343	P3/65	D16
587	1825	47.344	P3/65	D16
588	1826	47.345	P3/65	D16-D15
589	1827	47.346	P3/65	D16
590	1828	47.347	P3/65	D16
591	1829	47.348	P3/65	D16
592	1830	47.349	P3/65	D16
593	1831	47.350	P5/65	D16
594	1832	47.351	P5/65	D16
595	1833	47.352	P5/65	D16
596	1834	47.353	P4/65	D16-2E
597	1835	47.354	P5/65	D16
598	1836	47.355	P4/65	D16
599	1837	47.187	P5/65	5A
600	1838	47.188	P5/65	5A
601	1839	47.189	P4/65	5A
602	1840	47.190	P6/65	5A
603	1841	47.191	P5/65	5A
624	1862	47.212	5/65	41A
625	1863	47.213	5/65	41A
626	1864	47.214	5/65	41A
627	1865	47.215	5/65	41A
628	1866	47.216	5/65	41A
629	1867	47.217	5/65	41A
630	1868	47.218	5/65	41A
631	1869	47.219	6/65	41A

632	1870	47.220	6/65	41A	
633	1871	47.221	6/65	41A	
634	1872	47.222	6/65	41A	
635	1873	47.223	5/65	41A	
636	1874	47.224	6/65	41A	
637	1875	47.356	7/65	40B	
638	1876	47.357	6/65	41A	
639	1877	47.358	6/65	41A	
640	1878	47.359	6/65	41A	
641	1879	47.360	7/65	40B	
642	1880	47.361	2/66	41A	
643	1881	47.362	6/65	41A	
644	1882	47.363	7/65	40B	
645	1883	47.364	7/65	40B	
646	1884	47.365	7/65	40B	
647	1885	47.366	7/65	40B	
648	1886	47.367	8/65	40B	
649	1887	47.368	8/65	40B	
650	1888	47.369	7/65	41A	
651	1889	47.370	7/65	41A-52A	
652	1890	47.371	7/65	41A	
653	1891	47.372	8/65	41A	
654	1892	47.373	8/65	41A	
655	1893	47.374	8/65	40B	
656	1894	47.375	12/65	40B	
657	1895	47.376	9/65	41A	
658	1896	47.377	9/65	41A	
659	1897	47.378	9/65	41A	
660	1898	47.379	8/65	40B	
661	1899	47.380	8/65	40B	
662	1900	47.381	9/65	40B	
663	1901	47.225	9/65	86A	
664	1902	47.226	10/65	86A	
665	1903	47.227	9/65	86A	
666	1904	47.228	9/65	86A	
667	1905	47.229	9/65	86A	
668	1906	47.230	10/65	86A	
669	1907	47.231	9/65	86A	
670	1908		10/65	86A	(Accident Wdn. 8/69)
671	1909	47.232	10/65	86A	
672	1910	47.233	10/65	86A	
673	1911	47.234	10/65	86A	
674	1912	47.235	10/65	86A	
675	1913	47.236	10/65	86A	
676	1914	47.237	11/65	86A	
677	1915	47.238	12/65	86A	
678	1916	47.239	11/65	86A	
679	1917	47.240	12/65	86A	
680	1918	47.241	11/65	86A	
681	1919	47.242	11/65	86A	
682	1920	47.243	11/65	86A	
683	1921	47.244	12/65	86A	
684	1922	47.245	12/65	86A	
685	1923	47.246	12/65	86A	
686	1924	47.247	12/65	86A	
687	1925	47.248	12/65	86A	
688	1926	47.249	1/66	86A	
689	1927	47.250	1/66	82A	
690	1928	47.251	1/66	82A	
691	1929	47.252	2/66	82A	
692	1930	47.530	2/66	82A	
693	1931	47.254	2/66	82A	
694	1932	47.493	2/66	82A	
695	1933	47.255	3/66	82A	
696	1934	47.256	3/66	82A	
697	1935	47.257	3/66	82A	
698	1936	47.494	3/66	86A	
699	1937	47.495	4/66	86A	
700	1938	47.258	4/66	86A	
701	1939	47.496	P4/66	WL	
702	1940	47.497	P6/66	WL-D16	
703	1941	47.498	P7/66	WL	
704	1942	47.499	P6/66	WL-D16-WL	
705	1943	47.500	P7/66	WL	
706	1944	47.501	P7/66	WL	
707	1945	47.502	P7/66	D16	
708	1946	47.503	P7/66	D16	
709	1947	47.504	P7/66	D16	

610	1948 47.505	P8/66	WL	
611	1949 47.506	P9/66	WL	
612	1950 (47.259) 47.552	P9/66	WL	
613	1951 47.507	P11/66	WL	
614	1952 47.508	P11/66	WL	
615	1953 47.509	P12/66	WL	
616	1954 47.510	P12/66	WL-D16-WL	
617	1955 47.511	P12/66	WL-D16	
618	1956 47.260, 47.553	P13/66	WL	
619	1957 (47.261) 47.554	P1/67	WL	
620	1958 47.512	P2/67	WL	
621	1959 47.513	P2/67	WL	
622	1960 47.514	11/7/67	WL (DEC 67)	
623	1961 47.515	4/5/68	WL (MAY 68)	

Locomotive Depot Codes

2B	Nuneaton
2E	Saltley
5A	Crewe
16A	Toton
16C	Derby
D16	Nottingham Division
D15	Leicester Division
34G	Finsbury Park
40B	Immingham
41A	Tinsley
50A	York
52A	Gateshead
55A	Leeds (Holbeck)
64B	Haymarket
81A	Old Oak Common
82A	Bristol (Bath Road)
86A	Cardiff (Canton)
87E	Landore
WL	Western Lines of L.M.R.

The Works numbers of a few Brush type 4's have been out of sequence for a variety of reasons. For example, crossed identity at Falcon Works in error, delayed delivery and in the case of some D17XX examples sent to Derby for final paint, running nos. were applied in the sequence in which the locomotives were parked in the BR Yard. Some sources are at variance as to the actual identity but since many Brush plates have been removed positive identification may prove impossible. The list therefore depicts the probable order which was followed in the majority of instances.

Bracketed nos. indicate intended identification, which was not applied.

It must be noted that No. 361 was never used and the no. 443 was duplicated with an 0-4-0 shunter.

153. The crew of D 5500 surrender the token to the Grosmont signalman at the end of the 18-mile run from Pickering on the North Yorkshire Moors Railway. The locomotive is on loan to the NYMR from the National Railway Museum. The second and third coaches in the train are Gloucester-built DMU driving trailers temporarily rostered as 'hauled stock'.
A.M.Witton

THE TRANSPORT PUBLISHING COMPANY

The Transport Publishing Company has been in existence some four and a half years and is specialising in road transport history. A series of definitive histories of operators and manufacturers is being produced and a selection of current titles is shown below:-

The Leyland Bus. D. Jack.

We believe that this is the finest book about buses ever published and its record of the 2250 initial print order selling out in less than three weeks after publication makes it the most successful major book there has ever been in the transport field. Now reprinted, it tells the history of Leyland buses from their humble beginnings to the present position of the widest known maker of buses in the world. The superb pictorial coverage is a fitting counterpart to the comprehensive and authoritative text, for which the whole of Leyland's records were placed at the Author's disposal. pp. 440, with 716 photographs (2 of which are in full colour), 2 drawings and facsimiles of two advertising leaflets. Glindura-covered boards. 11¼ x 8.7/8''. SBN 903839 13 X. **£13.50**

Birmingham City Transport
Keeley, Russell, Gray

The history of the buses and trolleybuses in one of Britain's most advanced fleets. Nearly 500 pictures cover the period from pre-1914 to PTE. Colour illustrations and fold-out map included. A4 landscape, 8¼'' x 11¾''. SBN 903839 18 0. **£8.60**

Sheffield Transport. C.C. Hall.

Tracing as it does the development of road transport from the first record of pack mules in 1397 to April 1974, when Sheffield Corporation Transport became part of South Yorkshire PTE, we believe this is the finest account of how public road transport grew up in an urban area of Britain that has ever been compiled. This magnificent volume enshrines thirty years of careful research into local library records and Transport Department archives. Its detailed fleet lists of trams and buses will make it a must for enthusiast and historian alike. pp. 332, with 450 photographs (13 of which are in full colour); 7 portraits; a cartoon; facsimiles of 10 newspaper advertisements, 4 tokens and 31 tickets (29 in colour); 3 depot plans and 6 maps (2 of which are on a folding plate). "Fineweave" covered boards. Casebound. 11.7/8'' x 8.7/8''. SBN 903839 04 0. **£12.00**

Further details from The Transport Publishing Company, Glossop, Derbyshire.

TURNTABLE PUBLICATIONS

Brush Diesels has been published jointly with The Transport Publishing Company, but we also have a list of some fifty titles of our own of which the following are typical examples:-

The Post Office Railway London
Derek A. Bayliss
The first book which has ever been devoted to this fascinating and unique railway, a pioneer of automatic train control. The pneumatic tubes and railways of Victorian London which preceeded it are also fully described. pp.96 and 32 pages of plates; 3 maps and 2 scale drawings. Comprehensive bibliography and index. Case bound. 8½″ × 6″.
SBN 902844 43 1. **£3.50**

Station Master: My Lifetime's Railway Service in Yorkshire.
Len Bedale as told to C.T. Goode Rising from Lad Assistant, in the Outdoor Advertising Department, to Station Master, via Lampman, Porter, Shunter, Guard and Station Foreman, this autobiography gives a fascinating picture of working-class life and aspirations during the Depression and subsequent years, of interest to the railway enthusiast, social historian and general reader alike. pp. 80, with 44 photographs, 6 maps and 3 station track plans. Card covers, stapled sideways. 8¼ x 5.7/8″. SBN 902844 36 9. **£1.75**

Also available case bound. 8½″ x SBN 902844 38 5. **£2.**

Minimum Gauge Railways.
Sir Arthur Heywood.
The Author was the pioneer of the 15-inch gauge and the lines he laid out on his own estate at Duffield Bank, near Derby, and subsequently at Eaton Hall, Cheshire, were the forerunners of such well-known later ventures as the Ravenglass, Fairbourne, Romney, Hythe & Dymchurch and many other similar lines. His original book describing the laying out and running of very narrow gauge railways was never on general sale and only with this reprint has it become available to the public for the first time. The superb whole-page photographs alone make it worth a place in every enthusiast's library. pp. 59, and 23 plates. Casebound 10 x 7¼″ SBN 902844 26 1. **£2.85**

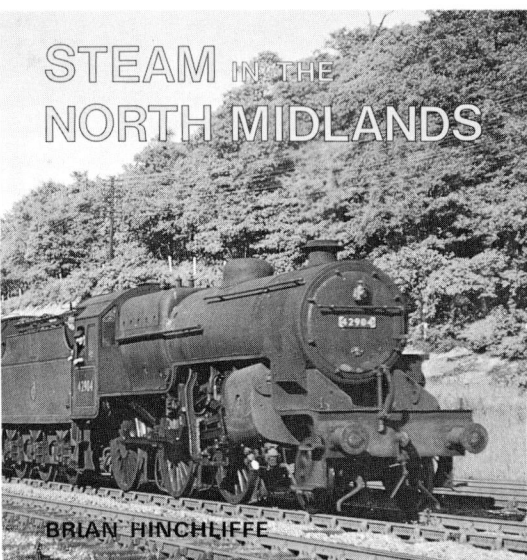

Steam in the North Midlands.
B. Hinchliffe.
Here for the first time is a photographic record of the main lines, branches and industrial scene in Sheffield and adjacent areas of South Yorkshire and North Derbyshire, in the last 40 years of the steam era. pp. 96, with 103 fine photographs, hitherto unpublished, by four talented local photographers. Casebound, with an eye-catching full-colour dust jacket. 8½ x 8¾″. SBN 902844 34 2. **£3.50**

Trams in German-speaking Countries/ Strassenbahnwagen in Deutsch-Sprachigen Ländern. R.J. Buckley.
The author traces the development of the tramca Continental Europe from the earliest electric ty to the most recent rapid-transport designs; the In duction and captions are printed in both English German. pp. 64, with 59 photographs. Card cov saddle-stitched. Oblong. 6 x 8½″. SBN 902844 39 3 **£1**

Complete catalogue from Turntable Publications, 745 Abbeydale Road, Sheffield.